Doing
Development
in Arkansas

Doing Development in Arkansas

Using Credit to Create
Opportunity for Entrepreneurs
Outside the Mainstream

RICHARD P. TAUB

The University of Arkansas Press
Fayetteville
2004

08   07   06   05   04   5   4   3   2   1

Designed by Ellen Beeler

⊗ The paper used in this publication meets the minimum requirements of the American National Standard for Permanence of Paper for Printed Library Materials Z39.48-1984.

Library of Congress Cataloging-in-Publication Data

Taub, Richard P.
   Doing development in Arkansas / Richard P. Taub.
      p. cm.
   Includes bibliographical references and index.
   ISBN 1-55728-776-7 (case bound : alk. paper)—ISBN 1-55728-778-3
   (pbk. : alk. paper)
   1. Rural development—Arkansas. 2. Arkansas Enterprise Group.
   I. Title.
HN79.A8T38 2004
307.1'412'09767—dc22

                                                        2004008915

The University of Arkansas Press gratefully acknowledges the generous support and contribution of the Winthrop Rockefeller Fondation in the publication of this book.

Contents

Illustrations

Figures

Tables

Acknowledgments

Funding for the research that produced this book came from the MacArthur, Ford, and Winthrop Rockefeller Foundations. Their representatives, Paul Lingenfelter, Lisa Mensah, Freeman McKendra, Sybil Hampton, and, toward the end, Bill Rahn, provided support, encouragement, and advice; and, in so doing, they were models of what foundation representatives should be.

Ronald Grzywinski, Mary Houghton, and George Surgeon, of the Shorebank Corporation and the Southern Development Bancorporation, shared information freely and encouraged the others in their organizations to do so in a manner unusual for chief executives. The other executives of Southern, Linda Chandler, Jeff Doose, Brian Kelly, Julia Vindasius, and Penny Penrose, were also gracious and helpful.

Although all of the Southern employees with whom I came into contact were helpful, Deborah Slayton, Bill Fowler, Todd Kirsten, Susan Maupin, and Stephanie McHenry made special efforts to make me understand their jobs and the people with whom they worked. They, along with Linda Chandler, took extra pains to teach me about Arkansas. Todd Kirsten taught me how to shoot, and Wali Mondal taught me how to fish.

Dean Bob Fisher, then dean of the Henderson State University School of Business, provided me with an office and arranged for me a place to stay when I was in town. Clayton Franklin, who was associated with the Business School Economic Development Center, showered me with ideas and insights. Both Henderson State and Ouachita Baptist University were facilitating in too many ways to count. The team members of the South Arkansas Rural Development Seminar—particularly Professors Hal Bass and Ray Grenade of Ouachita Baptist University, Jackie McCray of the University of Arkansas at Pine Bluff, Wali Mondal of Henderson State, the late Ruth Ann Tune from both OBU and Henderson, and Don Voth from the University of Arkansas in Fayetteville—were unending sources of information. Professor Voth is a particularly wise man and, as a fellow sociologist, was continually informative.

None of the research could have been completed without the assistance of Zina Murphy Bailey. Employed initially as a clerical person, she supervised the research operation in Arkansas, including overseeing survey researchers and student assistants. When she was required to take on additional responsibility, she cheerfully and competently did so. Rhonda St. Columbia, Iris Garza, and Shirley Davis supervised survey teams in distant locations.

George Surgeon, Alan Okagaki, Ning Wang, and my wife, Betty Farrell, were careful readers of an earlier version of the manuscript and had valuable suggestions. Christopher Horsch patiently explained legal matters to me.

I had had little experience of small town life before I began to spend time in Arkadelphia. Residents there were unfailingly helpful, warm, and friendly. They made me appreciate and understand small town life in a way I had not done before.

My late wife, Doris L. Taub, encouraged me in a project that required me to be out town for substantial periods of time and served as an important sounding board for many of my observations. She died before the research part of this project was completed.

CHAPTER 1

A New Approach to Development in Arkansas

In 1986, Arkansas governor Bill Clinton invited a northern, inner-city, development banking corporation to consider coming south to rural Arkansas in order to try its hand at rural economic development. By so doing, he set into motion a series of steps that resulted in Arkansas's largest foundation, the Winthrop Rockefeller Foundation, investing $5 million to help finance the move, accompanied by major investments and grants from the Ford and MacArthur foundations, bringing the total to $12 million. The move also played an important role in advancing the development of an important new industry among credit-granting institutions entitled Community Development Financial Institutions (CDFIs), which was undergirded by a new government agency with an annual budget of approximately $100 million and supported by major commitments from the Ford and MacArthur foundations as well as private sector-players. "A recent study of these organizations identified 900 certified CDFI's with an estimated $11 billion, minimum, in total assets" (Pinsky 2004). This is probably an underestimate due to difficulties in identifying the appropriate institutions.

This is the story of the Southern Development Bancorporation (Southern), a company created in rural Arkansas to upgrade the economy of the southern half of the state by using credit to encourage entrepreneurship and business development. Its progenitor, surprisingly, was the Shorebank Corporation, a Chicago bank-holding corporation that had achieved national recognition through its development efforts in the South Shore community, a minority area that had begun to decline in the late 1960s as part of the process of changing from a white to a minority community. The management of Shorebank had had a history of undertaking difficult tasks although the "smart money" viewed their efforts as quixotic. (Taub 1990). For example, they made the decision to buy a bank in the South Shore community of Chicago and invest there during a period, the early 1970s, when red-lining, the refusal of banks to make loans in communities they thought were in decline, and disinvestment were standard operating procedures of the city's banks. Through the use of credit and operating companies that had specialized development responsibilities, Shorebank was able to halt the economic decline of the community and improve the local economy.

Undertaking a superficially similar but in important ways quite different task in Arkansas was equally courageous. Shorebank had been successful in a major city in one of the most prosperous metropolitan areas in the United States. True, it had to deal with problems of disinvestment and other forces that led to neighborhood decline. However, major financial markets and other businesses were close by, so, in some sense, they merely had to redirect the flow of regional resources. The Arkansas story is a very different one. In Chicago's South Shore, the story was revitalization. In Arkansas, it was dealing with a long-term, very depressed economy.

Arkansas has long been on the list of the poorest states in the United States. On any list that measures incomes and their correlates, such as health, educational levels, and the like, Arkansas has always been near the bottom, its residents often grateful (so the saying goes) to Louisiana and Mississippi for usually being further down.

TABLE 1.1: MEDIAN HOUSEHOLD INCOME OF THE SIX POREST STATES			
STATE	INCOME	STATE	INCOME
West Virginia	$29,673	New Mexico	$33,124
Mississippi	$30,161	Louisiana	$33,322
Montana	$32,126	Arkansas	$33,339

Source: Adapted from the U.S. Bureau of the Census 1990, http://www.uscensus.gov.

Note: The percentages in poverty track these numbers quite closely.

TABLE 1.2: PERCENTAGE OF PEOPLE IN POVERTY IN THE SIX STATES WITH THE MOST POVERTY			
STATE	**% OF POOR**	**STATE**	**% OF POOR**
New Mexico	18.8	Arkansas	16.3
Louisiana	17.5	West Virginia	15.6
Mississippi	16.8	Texas	15.2

Source: Adapted from the U.S. Bureau of the Census 1990, http://www.uscensus.gov

Arkansas shares a pattern of Southern poverty that has deep roots. It is connected to the institutions of slavery and Jim Crow and to political and economic leaders who created conditions, including stingy expenditures on higher education, in order to maintain a system of low wages (Wright 1986). The South is also still largely, although not uniformly, rural and, with the exception of Atlanta, has produced few great cosmopolitan cities. Yet, the metropolitan areas with the great cities at their core have been the major locations for generating wealth in the United States.

Intervention in order to improve economic conditions is difficult in an economy with a thin and widely dispersed population with low educational levels. This is not an essay on the South. But it is important, when focusing on Arkansas's economic difficulties, to see that many of its problems are not merely problems of the particular state, but, rather, part of the pattern of a region that includes the old cotton plantation world of the Mississippi Delta, repeatedly identified as one of the poorest sections of the United States, with poverty rates in some areas of close to 50 percent and unemployment rates in the double digits. Indeed, Governor Clinton had contacted the Shorebank Corporation after an economic development conference in his state that was pessimistic about the economic future and compared Arkansas to a third world country. At the conference, somebody suggested that maybe the South Shore Bank people, who had had such dramatic results in helping to revitalize an inner-city community in Chicago, could do something.

Yet, even in Arkansas, there are dramatic examples of economic success that stand in contrast to the general picture. Unlike the Delta along

Arkansas's eastern border, which is flat and was ideal for plantation agriculture, the northwest region of the state is hilly and rocky and not particularly conducive to large-scale agriculture. Consequently, unlike in much of the rest of the state, slavery and a large African American population were never part of that region's history.

Nonetheless, beginning in the 1970s, northwestern Arkansas began to surmount the set of rural problems long associated with a history of low incomes and underemployment. Today, Northwest Arkansas has unemployment rates as low as almost any place in the United States. The engine for this growth came from the rise of old-fashioned entrepreneurship. Entrepreneurial leaders include Sam Walton, who founded his WalMart Stores there; John Tyson, the founder of a chicken empire; and J. B. Hunt, who moved there to grow one of the nation's largest trucking companies.

That success is unusual for two reasons. The first is that, unlike most of the fortunes created by entrepreneurs in the last quarter of the twentieth century—fortunes that came from the rise of the "new economy," such as the technology associated with Silicon Valley in California and Boston's Route 128 in Massachusetts—these were built on old-fashioned basic businesses: retail sales, the provision of poultry, and trucking. To be sure, all were quick to identify the advantages of modern information technology. WalMart may have been the first among major retailers to make use of satellites to speed information from stores to suppliers and to coordinate activities, for example; and they have all been very sophisticated in using the products of the information revolution to make their companies efficient. Second, Northwest Arkansas appears to violate the rules that some economic development experts might lay down as a necessary foundation. It had little of the kinds of infrastructure that development specialists say are needed to do development. The region lacked major highways and major airports. It is not in any center of population, with its closest city being Tulsa, Oklahoma, seventy miles away. It was not close to any stop on the information highway. It did (and still does) have a land-grant university, but did not have a particularly well-educated population. And it was not near a center of finance.

What the region did have were entrepreneurs who were smart and determined. And they started businesses that sometimes seemed unlikely to succeed in that location. For example, when Sam Walton decided to enter the discount store business, the consensus was that, without large markets nearby, he could not possibly generate the level of volume in sales he would need to succeed. Nevertheless, WalMart grew to be the world's largest retailer. In retrospect, one can make a case that the isolated rural location provided an advantage. One could argue that because the area was so unpromising, there was little competition from the existing big national chains, which gave Walton time to try different approaches outside the path of national retailers, who did not see this rural upstart as a threat. But that would have to be a retrospective argument, for general theory would suggest that, without real competition, such a company would never have to run at maximum efficiency. Walton also had access to credit. His wife was the daughter of a banker, and that banker provided loans to Walton when he was getting his business underway. In subsequent times, the Stephens Company, a large investment firm in Little Rock, stepped in with capital at crucial moments, such as when WalMart had grown too quickly and was overextended.

John Tyson was not near markets either. But he figured out how to get his perishable product, live chickens, to distant markets. At that time, local chickens could only be shipped successfully by truck during the summer as far as St. Louis. To increase his range, he used blocks of ice and fans to keep chickens alive and, consequently, fresh while carrying them to large and distant markets, such as the city of Chicago. Unlike the story of WalMart, where there were no obvious advantages to starting up in such a location, one can see with the poultry business that, once the transportation problem is solved, its success is linked to the presence of low-income, rural locations. Land for the chicken houses is cheap in Northwest Arkansas, and low-income farmers will put in the labor for low wages if that is what makes it possible for them to keep their farms. Rural areas are also more able and accustomed to dealing with the kinds of smells that chicken production generates. We do not have information about how the trucking industry grew in this isolated area without a major highway and with winding mountain roads providing access in some directions. But many areas of the rural South have provided truck drivers in disproportionate numbers because it was a way of finding jobs in a low-wage region, and the need for those jobs made drivers willing to stay on the road.

Although the key issue in southwestern and eastern Arkansas was poverty and not economic success, it is important to see how Northwest Arkansas provides a vision and a goal for other rural areas. It provides a useful comparative example of how a group of entrepreneurs economically transformed a region that had little going for it either in infrastructural or human capital (that is, an educated populace) terms. It suggests that, if one can find the tools in other poor regions to encourage the growth of entrepreneurship or to unleash natural talent, perhaps that talent can lead to economic growth.

It is not a pipe dream, then, that encouraging entrepreneurship can lead to economic growth, even in unlikely locales. There are additional arguments for using that particular path. For example, the attraction of branch plants of large corporations has been a development strategy for many poor states. However, there is persuasive evidence that those plants seldom produce enough revenue to pay back the incentives used to get them to move. Indeed, many pick up and move again once those incentives are exhausted. Furthermore, most of the jobs that pay well in those plants go to outsiders who come with the plants or are recruited nationally. In this argument, the low-wage jobs available to the local population do not have upgrade paths and do not provide opportunity for local people to improve their positions. Locally grown companies, it is argued, are more likely to see that the rewards for success remain local; and, in addition, such companies provide opportunities for local people who might be forced to leave the state otherwise. "Growing from the inside" is an appealing slogan. Although many economic development specialists put their faith in the development of human capital through education, at the state level the logic of that does not seem so unassailable, because it is also true that most of the educated population then must leave the state to go elsewhere for better opportunities.

Finally, the encouragement of entrepreneurship has a special attraction to Americans whose value system includes a commitment to independent effort and business growth.

Those who see entrepreneurship as the road to development also bring with them a theory about how to encourage both entrepreneurship and business growth. Their argument is that business growth has been crippled by a lack of access to credit, which is believed to be essential for both business startups and expansion. And that capital, maybe combined with some other things, will encourage entrepreneurship and the growth of smaller businesses, which will lead to economic development.

According to those theories, this kind of finance may not be available for several reasons. The first is outright discrimination or prejudice by the bankers who make loans. This is a particularly serious issue when one considers the plight of minorities, particularly African Americans and particularly in the South. There is a whole literature on the impact of lack of access to credit by African Americans both in housing and in business (Bates 1993; Aldrich and Zimmer 1986).

Another explanation is that rural banks have traditionally made what might be called "character loans." Bankers know the people involved so intimately and so well, often through several generations, that they feel certain about their credit worthiness. As one banker said to me about a particular loan applicant, "I know that family. They would always pay back a loan. They would work night and day and scramble in every way possible in order to scrape up the money to make their payments." The problem with character loans is that, if one does not know the people involved, one does not make the loan. And a banker may not make the effort to develop impersonal measurement tools to make loans on an analytic basis using cash flow, assets, business projections, and the like in a systematic way. There are variations on this story. Local bankers may not make credit widely available because they have an interest in keeping local populations in their place while maintaining their own positions of power. In this process, they may collude with other important people in the community. They may also use credit availability as a means of keeping potential dissidents in line.

A third layer of explanation is that southern banks, particularly, have been historically conservative and have chosen to invest in financial instruments rather than to make loans. There is evidence that, in fact, the loan-to-asset ratios of southern banks, particularly in non-urban settings, have been lower than they are nationally. One should add that, in the case of the Southern Development Bancorporation story, this was part of the thinking in 1988. Since then, the bank industry has changed massively in several ways, the most obvious of which is the decline of independent local banks and the consolidation of the banking industry into a relatively few national corporations. The literature is mixed on the consequences of credit provision at the local level; however, at the very least, it is clear that formal systems of evaluation reduce the effect of individual discretion in making loans.

The reader should keep in mind that the theory we are discussing has three steps to the analysis. The first has to do with the availability of credit. The second has to with the importance of credit in encouraging entrepreneurship and business growth. And the third step is that the building of local business capacity will also build the local economy. Implicit in this analysis is that, if the first three steps are taken, the economic gains will be distributed in such a way that those further down the economic ladder will also benefit. In the story we are considering, there is overwhelming evidence that African Americans have been discriminated against in credit markets. The evidence for each of the subsequent individual steps in the process is sparse or nonexistent.

There are three arguments that could be made against the possible success of any intervention at all. The first is the belief that entrepreneurs are "born" and not made, that there is some combination of drive, creativity, understanding of the business process, and desire for independence that either people have or they do not. This could be an explanation of why particular ethnic groups, such as Jews, overseas Chinese, and Parsis, Jains, and Marwaris in India, lead in entrepreneurial activities. It is for this reason that, until recently, most business schools placed little emphasis on entrepreneurial training.

A second argument against intervention is that, if the structure of economic opportunity is clear enough, entrepreneurs will come forward. This is a common argument put forward to explain the growth of Silicon Valley–type situations.

The third argument is that regions have comparative advantages and that economic activity will be organized around those advantages. From this perspective, labor should migrate from places with few advantages to those areas with more. Thus, it follows that interventions in places with no natural comparative advantage will automatically fail.

To some extent, the jury is still out on all of these perspectives. It would be difficult to find a comparative advantage in Northwest Arkansas, except in retrospect. And there is only the existence of one large, natural experiment—where the Finnish government transformed a mainly agricultural economy into an industrial one, partly through the encouragement of entrepreneurial activity (Santakallio 1998; Eräheimo and Laakso 2000).

Nonetheless, it was with that set of theories in mind, which related credit opportunities to regional development, that the state of Arkansas and the Winthrop Rockefeller Foundation informally invited the Shorebank Corporation of Chicago to come to Arkansas, buy a bank, and, with the bank and other kinds of resources, contribute to the economic growth of southern and eastern Arkansas. The Shorebank Corporation had already achieved a record of success in the South Shore neighborhood of Chicago by using credit and other tools to reverse an economic slide that followed upon racial turnover in that area (Taub 1988, 1994). Its bank subsidiary, the South Shore Bank, along with other related companies, had been able to attack the historic pattern of disinvestment, or "red-lining," which usually accompanied racial change in northern urban areas and, later, suburban areas. Its major tool was, indeed, credit, and, by providing it, the South Shore Bank was filling a niche abandoned by conventional banks whose owners believed that, when neighborhoods change racially, they began an inexorable downward slide, which would cause the lenders to lose their money.

The bank began its efforts by providing mortgages for single-family homes and then, subsequently, extending credit to African American landlords or would-be landlords who wanted to upgrade property in order to supplement their income with small rental units. In addition, one of the Shorebank Company's subsidiaries entered directly into the housing market, using an array of subsidy programs to take larger, neglected buildings, fix them up, and rent them to local residents.

The South Shore Bank's success, then, was mainly in shoring up the housing market and, by so doing, making it possible for a group of small investors to increase their income by purchasing and rehabilitating housing. In the city of Chicago, the South Shore community is primarily a bedroom community. Historically, its residents were employed in the once-great steel mills to the south and east, or downtown, either in business or government or corporate offices. Consequently, it was not the sort of area in which to focus on industrial or business growth. And most of the South Shore Bank's contribution to strengthening the area did not come from that sector. The South Shore Bank had, in fact, tried to lend money for local retail business development, but it was not visibly successful in that effort. In fact, in the business area, its biggest achievement was the assembly of property for a large, in-city strip mall, anchored by a major super market chain and leased up by national corporations with local outlets. The move to Arkansas therefore represented a departure from the major thrust and the major successes of the corporation's activities in Chicago.

But members of Shorebank's management considered their work with landlords, which included close supervision and technical assistance, also to be entrepreneurial development. In addition, they had become familiar with business development programs, particularly those that used credit tools, in other parts of the world. They had worked closely with the famous Grameen Bank in Bangladesh (more about this below), which made very small loans to poor peasants so that they could start small businesses. They had visited successful business development programs in Finland and in the Scottish Highlands. They had some clear idea about what worked and what did not in a diverse array of settings.

So, supported by the Winthrop Rockefeller Foundation in Arkansas, which courageously invested approximately $5 million and provided grant funds as well; by other local foundations and investors, including the Walton Family Foundation; and by national organizations, including the MacArthur, Ford, and Mott foundations, the Shorebank team established a company in Arkansas.

The beginning of this story, then, is the genesis of the Southern Development Bancorporation and the theory that lay behind its genesis. We see a Northern urban development company, with banking at its center, invited by the governor and the major foundation in the state to encourage economic growth in a Southern rural state—and to do so with an approach that was in many ways untested. Nobody could be sure that such an effort could succeed. But experts offered little hope that anything else would either. The state had already put in place a whole array of development activities. These included efforts at attracting branch plants of large corporations with the use of subsidies, economic development centers where specialists offered some kind of technical assistance, and programs to encourage the growth of science and technology activities. In that spirit, it is important to see this effort as an experiment and as a learning process. It represented a new approach where so many other attempts had produced limited success. Unfortunately, as we shall see, the notion of this as an experimental effort was somewhat lost under the pressures of implementation, as all the participants—Shorebank, foundations, and politicians—tended to oversell the enterprise, and the inevitable publicity that followed tended to treat the whole story as a success before it even started.

In any situation where a group or an organization operates in the public sphere, there is some distance between what is planned and what actually happens. People and organizations are not cogs in a machine where one pushes a button and all whirs in careful pre-programmed order. In the implementation of any program, one must confront the intractabilities of the real world. Larger social forces intervene in unpredictable ways. Individuals have their own interests and concerns; organizations develop their own agendas. There is a large literature in the study of implementation that has a rueful quality, as great ideas topple when confronted by the real world. The most famous book on this subject is subtitled *How Great Expectations in Washington Are Dashed in Oakland [CA] —Why It Is Amazing That Federal Programs Work at All* (Pressman and Wildavsky 1984). Southern's effort was not a federal program, but an unusual combination of for-profit and not-for-profit activity with some government tie-ins. But, as an organization with goals to alter the larger society—in this case through economic development—it has problems in common with those federal programs. With this perspective in mind, and the brief background history, I turn to what actually transpired in southern Arkansas, stopping from time to time to discuss the lessons learned in the process.

CHAPTER 2

The Organization of Southern and Its Divisions

As I have suggested, there is some distance from the development of an idea to its implementation as a program. As one moves from the world of abstraction and planning to the process of actually doing, one has to make compromises with what the real world has to offer in order to move a plan from conception to actuality. What is striking sometimes is how very early steps and the decisions that have to be made have consequences for outcomes which are not obvious until much further down the road. Observing the confrontation with the real world in the process of simply putting Southern in place, we can see how decisions play out. Let me provide two examples.

The first has to do with the creation of the company itself. The Southern Development Bancorporation (Southern) was established not as a branch of Shorebank in Chicago, which had been part of the original plan, but, instead, because of limitations created by federal laws about branch banking, as a separate corporation with its own Arkansas-based board of directors. One consequence of this was a certain loss of autonomy for the Chicago-based management. In addition, having to recruit an Arkansas-based board was a different kind of proposition from what went into creating the Chicago board. Here we begin to see the consequences of a group of outsiders—that is, Chicagoans—trying to have an impact in a distant place. The Chicago board was created by management identifying people either with whom it had a previous, continuing relationship or through its networks of personal contacts. The result was a board made up of successful people from different walks of life, but people not at the apex of celebrity. They included, at various times, successful businessmen who had demonstrated a commitment to urban development issues, a former business school dean and investor, foundation officials, a nun who represented her community, a partner in a Big Eight accounting company. A few of them were near neighbors of the company's founder. As a group, they derived pleasure from participation on the board and felt that the experience enhanced them, while giving them an opportunity to participate in something they defined as worthwhile. It was not surprising to hear one or another of them say of their participation on the Shorebank board, "This is the best thing I do."

By contrast, when one parachutes into a new region, the opportunity to create a board through continuing personal contact is much reduced. In this particular case, board selection faced additional constraints. Shorebank was brought to Arkansas by the governor and the head of the state's largest foundation, making it a top-down entry. In addition, compared to economically stronger states, Arkansas has a small elite, reducing the number of solid upper-middle-class choices possible. The result was an Arkansas board that included people who might be counted as some of the leading figures in the state. These included Hillary Clinton, who was both the wife of the governor and a distinguished attorney, and Tom McRae, who, as the president of the Winthrop Rockefeller Foundation, had played a major role in bringing Shorebank to Arkansas. At one point, he also just happened to be a candidate for governor who had run against Hillary Clinton's husband in the Democratic primary. Other board members included Rob Walton, an attorney and the heir apparent to the Walton businesses and thus to the largest family fortune in the state; Walter Smiley, one of the state's leading high tech entrepreneurs, the founder of Systematics, which provided automated bookkeeping services for banks, and also a close associate of the Stephens Companies, venture capitalists, bank owners, and communications entrepreneurs; Donald Munro, founder and president of the Munro Shoe Company, Arkansas's sixth largest privately owned company and an important supplier to WalMart; and Walter Patterson, an African American, who had headed the Department of Human Services in Arkansas. Subsequently, Walton was represented by Stewart Springfield, who was the head of the Walton Family Foundation. In contrast to the Chicago group, these people felt that they lent luster to the company by coming onto the board in the way that big names lend themselves to charitable activities. From the beginning, their participation on the board did not have the same standing in their lives that it did for members of the Chicago board. The Arkansas board members, as natives, could have facilitated entry into the state , but they failed to do so. Only one board member worked hard to raise capital, for example, and only one ever opened an account in Southern's Elk Horn Bank. They were too far removed from the local community and the bank's clients to help generate business. By contrast, the members of the board of Shorebank's Cleveland branch helped raise deposits for the bank and facilitated working relationships with the city government.

The board and management of Southern never developed the same kind of close and trusting working relationship in which there was easy communication that had characterized the Chicago board. My own observation was that Southern officials often seemed to be working hard to sell their achievements to a skeptical audience. By contrast, the Shorebank board identified with the company and shared in the pride of management's achievements.

To be sure, relationships like this grow from mutuality. Some of the Southern board members also felt that Shorebank managers did not put enough effort into building personal ties with them. In a way that had symbolic meaning, the top Shorebank officials, who had perhaps been catapulted into the national scene by the Clinton connection at a time when they were involved in expansion of the Shorebank companies to other states, flew in and out of Little Rock for meetings and were not perceived to invest much effort in building the kinds of social ties that were part of the southern way of doing things, characterized (although too simplistically) as participating in the "old boys' network." One board member discussed this explicitly: "After one board meeting, I heard them (management) talking among themselves about where they were going to go to dinner. I thought to myself, we should all be discussing this and going out together." Another board member, not one of the celebrities and a later addition, reported that she wondered why she was at meetings since nobody ever asked her opinion about anything. Shorebank's management also had an array of activities underway that helped cause those quick visits. Indeed, much later in the process at a crucial meeting, management's participation had to be arranged by speakerphone.

Social relations of this sort become difficult to alter once negative processes are set in motion. But the point of the story is that both groups did not work together well. In Arkansas, this was a particularly serious issue because, as I shall discuss below, there were important ways that Arkansas was closed to "outsiders," and an active, supportive board could have helped to clear the way. This also presages the denouement of this story when the Chicago team left Arkansas, and the Southern board more directly took on responsibility for managing the company.

The second early accident that helped to shape future outcomes involved the purchase of a bank. As in Chicago, Southern officials wanted to create a holding company that had a for-profit, regulated bank at its center. The first task, then, was to find a bank that would serve as its core institution, as it had in Chicago. Learning from its experience in Chicago, where the first years included shoring up a shaky institution that had been under-maintained because its owners hoped to sell and relocate the bank, the organization, to the great frustration of its board, took more than a year to find a good bank. The first segment of the search took place in eastern Arkansas, the Delta, where, historically, plantation agriculture had been its economic center and where, as in other parts of the South, a large minority population was mired in poverty—with poverty rates sometimes as high as a third.

That effort proved fruitless. Banks for sale either were not in very good financial condition or came hedged with undesirable conditions, such as keeping relatives of the original owners employed. And, in some cases, there was community pressure from local leaders against selling the bank, one of the sources of elite power in the community, to a group of outsiders, especially from as far away as Chicago. There is a story told about one bank whose owner came close to selling, but who abandoned the idea when community leaders offered to buy him out rather than let him surrender local control.

This state of affairs was frustrating to the board, whose members wanted to get started. Shortly after Southern had been created, one of the directors complained, "I have never seen such cautious and risk-averse people." Finally, a bank became available. Unfortunately, for the way things played out, it was not in the depressed eastern part of the state, but rather in the southwest. This came about because a banker in the southwest offered his bank for sale. It was no secret in Arkansas that there was a Chicago group in search of a bank. Getting reports of the failed search, the owner of the Elk Horn Bank in Arkadelphia, the seat of Clark County and a town in southwestern Arkansas, offered his bank for sale. A successful real estate developer, he had purchased the bank when its former owner had fallen on hard times. The bank was an economic success, but downtown Arkadelphia was following the path of other small towns into serious decline. There were two reasons for this. One was the migration of business activity out to the "mall," which, in this case, was mainly a WalMart store and a few supermarkets. And the other was the fact that Arkadelphia itself was going through an economic crisis.

Some of the area's largest manufacturers and major employers had closed their doors in the early 1980s, leaving an unemployment rate of 15 percent. These companies included Reynolds Aluminum, with a large array of facilities in Clark County and in neighboring counties. In addition, there had been a ball-bearing factory and a cut-and-sew operation of Levi Strauss.

The Elk Horn owner had remodeled the bank and the adjacent building, but the changes had little impact. Things became so bad downtown that "grass was growing in the cracks in the sidewalk." He decided that he could not do any more for the downtown area, and, besides, he was getting ready to sell the bank. Before he made the move, he did check with other local leaders, including the owner of another bank in town. He thought that maybe these newcomers had ideas worth trying and, in addition, he had pressing uses for the money he would get from the sale of the bank with its $50 million in assets.

Although Arkadelphia was approximately 150 miles from where the Shorebank people ideally preferred to be, the Southern board members were getting impatient waiting for a bank purchase. In addition, Arkadelphia as a town had several distinct advantages from management's perspective. The first was that it was a university town. Both Henderson State University, a former teacher's college with about 3,000 students, and Ouachita (pronounced Washata) Baptist University, with about 1,200 students, and the faculty and administrative staffs of each, were located there, providing some level of economic stability or a floor below which the community was unlikely to fall.

The presence of the two universities contributed to making the town more cosmopolitan than many Arkansas towns and publicly more racially tolerant than some other towns of similar size. The assistant superintendent of the schools was black, even though the school was majority white. Black members sat on the board of the Clark County Industrial Council, and community leaders made a self-conscious effort to be modestly inclusive.

One community leader, in fact, pointed out that, when doing industrial recruiting, it was important to have visible minority members on public boards. Companies interested in relocating were likely to have some nonwhite employees and would want to see to it that they would be comfortable in town. It was also true, however, that Arkadelphia had a much smaller minority population—less than 25 percent—than did those Delta towns where African Americans were in the majority.

At any rate, from the perspective of the Shorebank Company, which had African American executives and envisioned having even more of them in Arkadelphia and which had defined improving the plight of black Americans as a major part of their mission, the relative openness to diversity in Arkadelphia was an important issue.

Finally, downtown Arkadelphia was three miles from a major interstate highway. This made it easily accessible to Shorebank officials who would be flying into Little Rock, which, at that time, contained the only airport in the state which received the jet airplanes of the major carriers and was, at seventy miles, an hour's drive away.

It contained also a local family with a small foundation that contributed to civic betterment. The Ross Foundation supported a program to help the two universities work together; for example, it sponsored lectures and musical performances (unusual in many small towns) and provided money to help the Clark County Industrial Council at a difficult juncture in its financing. In short, although it was not an ideal location for dealing with Arkansas's most serious poverty or for addressing the concerns of Governor Clinton and some of Southern's board members, it had advantages. And the bank was available. Nonetheless, it was another of those early decisions that had fateful consequences. The town was so far from the most depressed part of the state that the organization felt continual pressure, some self-generated and some external, to become involved in development activities in the Delta region. To the extent that the company made an effort to do so, it greatly stretched slender resources and the capacity for supervision.

Another consequence of the decision was that the Elk Horn Bank faced the unusual problem for a town of this size of having two other competitor banks and two branches of statewide savings and loan associations in this town of mostly low- and moderate-income citizens. For most of the time of this study (1988–97), the major competing bank was owned by the same old and important local family that operated the foundation mentioned above. Another was headed by a board member of Ouachita Baptist University (OBU), one of the two colleges in town. Not only was the Elk Horn Bank going to have to generate development activity, but its management would have to consume energy, time, and resources competing with the other local financial institutions for deposits and for good loan customers. During the course of the study, Elk Horn also built two branches, one on the edge of town, out near the interstate highway we described above, which was emerging as a growing business area, and another in a rapidly growing town nearby (the growth due, it was said, to white flight from Arkadelphia and another nearby town, Malvern), as it struggled to stay even with competitors who were not standing idle either. One of the competitors constructed a branch in that same town. And later, during this period, the same company rebuilt its old building, taking over a whole city block by constructing the most imposing structure in downtown Arkadelphia. Although ultimately the com-peting banks were sold to larger bank chains, in the early years they emphasized in their advertising that they were *local* banks and people would be better off doing business with them.

I will return to the story of Arkadelphia in more detail subsequently.

The Structure of Southern

With bank ownership in place as Southern's centerpiece, the time had come to construct the rest of the organization. Given its modest endowment, the organization's structure, modeled on the structure of the Shorebank Company in Chicago, was quite intricate. The intricacy was heightened by the fact that the informal structure of the organization—that is, how it operated on a daily basis—did not reflect the formal structure, and this contributed to tension among the company's various elements. Indeed, that complexity is another of those early decisions that had consequences for the effective functioning of the company later on. I will discuss the way the structure actually worked in practice during the early years and then the organization's legal structure, and why the differences between the two created confusion.

As was the case for the Shorebank Corporation in Chicago, the Southern Development Bancorporation was a one-bank holding company. Its one bank was the Elk Horn Bank. Again, like Chicago, it included a second subsidiary, the Opportunity Lands Corporation, which was a for-profit real estate development company. In its early phases, Opportunity Lands differed from its Chicago equivalent in that its focus was to be on office space development and business incubators. The Chicago equivalent's major focus was on housing development.

The structural story gets a little more complicated at this point. Part of the Southern package included a not-for-profit affiliate, the Arkansas Enterprise Group (AEG). As a matter of law, AEG was created as a sepa-rate company, since for-profit banks cannot normally be partnered with not-for-profit companies. If they were, there would be an incentive to use the not-for-profit company in illicit ways to maximize the profits of the for-profit company or to launder or hide taxable dollars.

On the other hand, management believed that a not-for-profit like this was essential to a development program. Only not-for-profits are eligible for foundation grants, an important source of funds for operating budgets. In addition, there is an array of government programs that aim to make grants and loans to not-for-profit organizations. Resources like these make

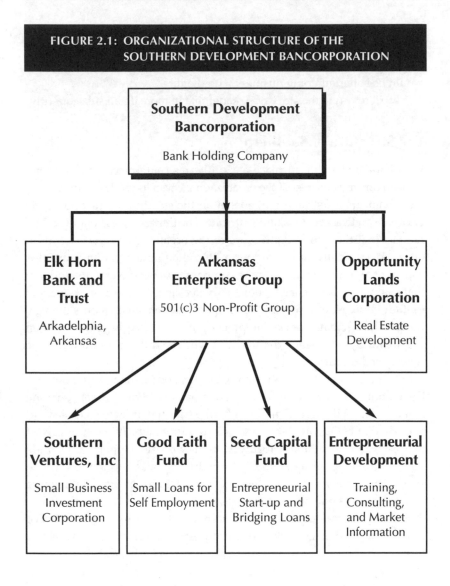

FIGURE 2.1: ORGANIZATIONAL STRUCTURE OF THE SOUTHERN DEVELOPMENT BANCORPORATION

it possible to subsidize development activities that are not profitable from the straight business standpoint. For example, banks obviously have a fiduciary responsibility to their investors and depositors. In addition, banks are regulated and subject to frequent examination. Consequently, they are not supposed to make risky loans. A not-for-profit, by contrast, might be encouraged to take more chances as it encourages nascent businesses. In addition, a development organization might engage with the public in ways that do not yield revenue, but that do contribute to successful development outcomes. Providing technical assistance to young companies might be one example. Organizing business fairs, which encourage perspective entrepreneurs, might be another. Establishing cooperative marketing organizations might be yet another. Such activities might garner support from foundations or federal programs aimed at not-for-profits that perceive that such activities will ultimately promote economic well-being for a region or group. I will come back to this aspect of organizational structure subsequently, because it became a source of confusion about management responsibility.

The point here is that the Southern effort included a combination of for-profit and not-for-profit organizations. But as it told its story to potential funders, Southern marketed itself as one enterprise, and early organization charts (see figure 2.1) showed it as one enterprise. But it is important to bear in mind that legally the whole operation required two organizations, with the not-for-profit being a separate company from Southern and being governed by its own board. Central management (that is, Shorebank) considered the whole Southern enterprise as one. Yet it was clear that AEG's manager sometimes acted as if he were part of Southern and, at other times, as if there were two organizations, and he was the manager of a freestanding enterprise, which, in fact, legally he was.

To further complicate this complex organizational structure, AEG was divided into three divisions. They were called AEG Manufacturing Services (AMS), Southern Ventures, and the Good Faith Fund. As one can see in figure 2.1, the Arkansas Enterprise Group was originally conceived as having four components. However, what happened in practice was that the Seed Capital Fund and the Entrepreneurial Development program were managed as a single unit, which, in effect, became AMS.

Although these subdivisions were organized as subordinates under the AEG umbrella, for most of their lives they functioned as three equal units, each with its own manager. Let us now turn to each of these.

DIVISION #1: SOUTHERN VENTURES

The first of these was Southern Ventures, a venture capital company. As a venture capital company, its task was to find promising businesses, either as start-ups or as companies needing capital to move up to a new level, and to become investors in them. Southern Ventures' initial level of funding was $1,200,000. Established as something called a Small Business Development Corporation (SBDC), there was hope that this fund would be augmented by loan funds from the Small Business Administration in a program to fulfill its mandate. However, this relationship produced far fewer resources than were anticipated.

It is important to note here that venture capital companies relate to clients and potential clients in ways quite different from banks. Banks make loans. Loans are structured to minimize risk. In order to do this, not only do banks make an analysis of business plans, cash flow, and the like, but also they usually require collateral, either in cash or equities or in buildings and equipment, so that if the borrower cannot meet his or her obligations, the bank will get its money back or, at least, a major part of it. The other fact about loans as compared to investments is that they generally are for a fixed rate of interest, and they are accompanied by a payment schedule. A good bank tries to keep its bad loans below 1 percent. Banks are lending the money of their depositors, and, because of that and the fact that the government insures these deposits, they are also subject to government oversight and examination. Bank examiners rate banks, among other measures, by their loan portfolio quality, collateral adequacy, and loan loss reserves. If these are not up to the proper standard, they lose their charter.

Venture capital companies, by contrast, mainly make investments rather than loans. Investments are equity or ownership positions, and, to the extent that that is true, venture capital firms become partners in the businesses in which they participate. If those companies are profitable, the investor shares in the profits equal to his or her proportion of its ownership. If the business does not earn profits, the investor does not get any return. If the business fails, the venture capitalist loses his or her investment. As one can see, this is unlike the situation we have described concerning bank loans, where businesses pay back the loans until all resources are depleted. Indeed, business borrowers are frequently required to make personal guarantees as well, so that, if the business as a corporation cannot pay its debts, the bank can recover funds from the owners' personal wealth. Venture capital investments are not usually collateralized.

The pure venture capital investment, then, is riskier than a bank loan. On the other hand, by not being restricted to a fixed rate of return, a venture capital company can earn large sums of money if the object of its investment shows dramatic profitability. Economic theory suggests that the more risk there is, the higher the rate of return has to be in order to attract investors. This is reflected in the fact that venture capitalists expect that, although some of the companies they invest in will fail—perhaps even more than those who succeed—their successes, if they select well, will become very profitable, much more so than just making up for the losses. In summary, then, venture capitalists, looking at one investment prospect at a time, function in a higher risk environment than do bankers.

There is also a difference in how bankers and venture capitalists think about the relationship of time to money. The returns from a young, small business are much slower to materialize for a venture capitalist than loan income is for a banker. When a banker makes a loan, he or she receives regular monthly payments of some combination of interest and principal. By contrast, a small or growing company may take many years to become at all profitable, and even longer to become dramatically so. Under this scenario, until the business has profits to share, there is no revenue coming to the venture capitalist. To be sure, there may be good outcomes from the point of view of the venture capitalist before the company becomes truly profitable. The target company may get a new infusion of capital from somewhere else and decide to buy out its original equity provider at a good profit. Or some outside company may want to purchase the fledgling company and pay its owners handsomely to do so. But, nonetheless, returns take longer to materialize for the venture capitalist than for the bank loan officer. One can also see from this discussion that the pattern of cash flow is quite different in each case, with the new venture capitalist having to wait some time to take in operating funds, much less profits.

As owners, venture capitalists approach their clients differently than bankers do. They may sit on boards and look over management's shoulders; and contracts are often written that make it clear that, if existing management does not achieve pre-agreed-upon goals, investors can step in, take charge, and even replace management. Bankers are not legally allowed to operate the companies in default and, more to the point, do not usually want to. In fact, there are some legal limits on how much advice bankers can offer. "Lender liability" becomes a legal problem if the banker seems excessively involved in providing business guidance and if his advice leads to economic failure.

To those who understand the world of banking and investment, these details may seem obvious. But I underscore this set of differences now, because, as we shall see, a company that includes bankers and venture capitalists will approach the issues of investing and lending quite differently, and this may have consequences for organizational functioning. Even if these differences are understood in the abstract, it may not be obvious how they work out on a day-to-day basis. And, indeed, the playing out of these differences had serious consequences for Southern.

Venture capital companies, it should be added, are not obligated to take only equity positions. They can make loans, too, particularly in the form of specialized kinds of debt. Sometimes they might assemble a mix of loans and investments so that the loan portion of a portfolio provides an income flow in early stages and also dilutes risk. Southern Ventures' manager was loath to make loans in his portfolio because he believed that it was only the effect of a major injection of capital without other financial obligations that would either get companies started or jump them up to a new level. In his view, starting a new company with large debt obligations places it at a handicap in most effectively allocating its resources. In addition to the hope that Southern Ventures would have Small Business Administration funds available to it, there was hope that other investors with development interests would add to Southern Ventures' resources. One member of the Walton family operated a venture capital company, and there was the hope that her unit would become involved. The state also operated capital funds for economic development whose managers expressed interest. Because of differences with the Small Business Administration about the use of loans as compared to investments, the SBA funds were not forthcoming. None of the other hopes were ever realized.

DIVISION #2: AEG MANUFACTURING SERVICES (AMS)

As can be seen in figure 2.2, AMS was what was left from the Arkansas Enterprise Group when Southern Ventures and the Good Faith Fund were excluded. (The reader is asked to remember that this description is how the companies actually worked for much of their lives, rather than how they were legally constructed.) AMS's purpose was to encourage small businesses with an array of tools. These included various forms of small loans, some of which were characterized as seed capital. It was also expected to provide technical assistance for fledgling businesses and to do anything else that would encourage business development. In the early days, there was some plan that this company could work with small manufacturing companies and nurture them with training and riskier loans than a bank would undertake until they were strong enough to go to a real bank, such as Elk Horn, for a bankable loan.

In its early conception, lending was to be only a small part of AMS's activity. An early document summarized AEG's (or, for the purpose of this discussion, AMS's) responsibilities: "AEG will house the corporation's principal capacities to support development initiatives. AEG is a technical assistance arm to provide accounting, business planning, marketing and other business management services to client companies. . . . A seed capital fund would make soft loans to promising entrepreneurs for product, management and marketing development" (Shorebank planning document

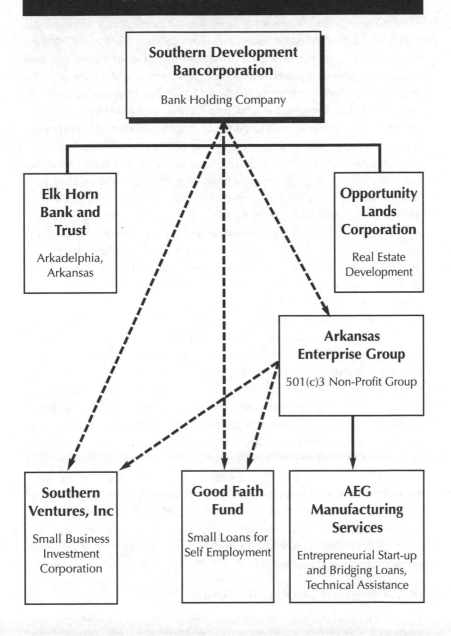

FIGURE 2.2: ORGANIZATIONAL RELATIONSHIPS AMONG THE COMPANIES OF THE SOUTHERN DEVELOPMENT BANCORPORATION

Southern Development Bancorporation

Bank Holding Company

Elk Horn Bank and Trust

Arkadelphia, Arkansas

Opportunity Lands Corporation

Real Estate Development

Arkansas Enterprise Group

501(c)3 Non-Profit Group

Southern Ventures, Inc

Small Business Investment Corporation

Good Faith Fund

Small Loans for Self Employment

AEG Manufacturing Services

Entrepreneurial Start-up and Bridging Loans, Technical Assistance

1987, 3). As we shall see, lending became AMS's major activity, with the other program components falling by the wayside.

The plan was that the non-lending component of the mandate could be financed by grant funds from foundations and government agencies. It is useful here to divide grant funds into two categories. One category is operating funds. That is, the foundation pays to cover the costs of running the company. The other is a pool of funds to be used for loans only, and which can then be recycled as loans are paid back. The distinction in the real world between operating funds and loan funds is not always this clear. For if the money to be lent arrives either as a grant or a very low interest loan, there is a profit to be made from the interest charged to the company's borrowers, which in some programs can then be used for operating purposes. At times, it has seemed as if foundation representatives and government officials thought that contributions to revolving loan funds could become a kind of perpetual-motion machine requiring no further subsidy, as the profits from loans would fund the ongoing operating of the company. But just as a perpetual-motion machine is an unrealistic dream, a self-perpetuating loan fund is also a highly unlikely structure. I will discuss this issue in more detail below. Suffice it to say that there is continuous pressure on these types of development organizations to approach self-sufficiency. This puts pressure on them to generate loan volume to produce income even if some of these deals are excessively risky.

AMS was under this kind of constant pressure to become self-supporting. It was also much more successful at accessing loan funds than it was at getting those to assist operations. Yet, the kind of lending it was supposed to do was of the most expensive sort—small business development in which owners might need help with making applications, keeping more sophisticated books than they thought they needed for day-to-day operations, and other forms of technical assistance. Under this kind of pressure, it tried to sell its technical assistance and other services to clients. That, as we shall see, is self-defeating. Because of the income pressures, staff size, and other matters to be discussed below, the technical assistance side of the AMS operation mostly withered away, except where the company it tried to save was in danger of sinking and taking loan dollars with it, in which case AMS stepped in to provide directly, in a one-on-one way, management assistance.

DIVISION #3: THE GOOD FAITH FUND

The most famous of AEG's subsidiaries was the Good Faith Fund. It began its life as a peer-group, micro enterprise, revolving loan fund that targeted very low income people and was modeled somewhat closely on the Grameen Bank of Bangladesh. Its was the most creative and courageous element of a creative operation.

The Grameen Bank is one of a group of organizations located mostly in the third world that are micro-credit, peer-group, lending organizations. With more than two million very poor rural customers in 1994 and a repayment rate in the high 90 percent range, it has become the most famous and widely imitated of such groups. Its distinguishing feature is the assembly of a small groups of borrowers who take turns getting the loans, with each member getting her/his opportunity when another has mainly paid hers/his off. The belief is that peer-group pressure sees to it that loans are repaid, so that others can take them. This is reputed to be an effective technique with poor people, who often do not have collateral to put up against loans.

In Bangladesh, such loans went frequently to people purchasing cows so they could sell milk to their neighbors or to the purchase of rice-hulling machines. But they could also be used for purchasing inventory for door-to-door peddlers or, more recently, for purchasing wireless telephones whose time could be rented to other members of the community. There are other features that are part of the Grameen Bank story. There are group meetings, for example, which are inspirational in nature, and group members commit themselves to patterns of behavior, such as growing vegetables, which are outside the loan and business orbit narrowly conceived. Nonetheless, the key features—peer-group process and very small loans for very small businesses—are the ones most widely imitated.

The first manager of the Good Faith Fund actually visited Bangladesh so that she would understand the fine points of the model, which could then be replicated in southern Arkansas. In fact, its adoption required numerous changes to fit the new habitat. In chapter 5, I shall discuss themes and variations as Good Faith Fund management tried to fine-tune the process for American and Arkansas locales. The important point for now is that the program began with the idea of making small loans, initially no more than two thousand dollars, with group processes helping to assure that the loans were repaid.

Unlike all of the other Southern companies that were located in Arkadelphia and, for most of their lives even in the same building, the Good Faith Fund was headquartered in Pine Bluff, a city about ninety miles to the east and almost a two-hour drive away.

Even though in decline, Arkadelphia had the characteristics of a charming rural town. But Pine Bluff, with a population of about sixty-five thousand people, was a seriously decayed city (at the time the only metropolitan statistical area in the state besides Little Rock), with a large minority population and some problems common to the urban poor. Arkadelphia had found its way onto one list of the best cities in which to raise children. By contrast, Pine Bluff was listed last in another report among a group of three hundred cities evaluated for their quality of life. At one of the entries to town is a large billboard announcing, "Jesus is the Answer for Pine Bluff." Visitors to town often pointed out that he would need a lot of help. Historically, the city served as an entryway and entrepôt to the southern section of the Arkansas Delta. Cotton dealers had lined its streets. It had been the headquarters of the old Cotton Belt railway line, which later became Southern Pacific. But, by the time the Good Faith Fund opened its doors there, the downtown was a decayed relic with mostly empty storefronts, retail activity having moved out to the mall, a high unemployment rate, and a clear pattern of white flight. The city's main employer was a huge International Paper factory, employing more than a thousand people, which produced much of the world's material for plastic-coated milk and juice containers. When the wind blew the wrong way, the factory's acrid smells enveloped the entire city. The county in which Pine Bluff is located also housed a state prison and a United States Government Center for Toxicological Research.

It is also the home of the University of Arkansas's Pine Bluff (UAPB) campus, a "historically black" college. Today, it is still a majority black institution, with a substantial proportion of its faculty and administration African American. According to informants, that largely middle-class group is cut off from the low-income African Americans, who comprise about half of the Pine Bluff population, and, of course, from the whites. During the time of this study, whenever the *Pine Bluff Commercial*, the local daily newspaper, listed the most important or powerful people in Pine Bluff, the UAPB president, regardless of who was filling that position, was usually the only black person on the list. It was clear that this was a symbolic act only. He did not have much real power in the community. So, the decision to locate the Good Faith Fund there grew out of the pressures I have already discussed to conduct some of Southern's activity in the Delta. Pine Bluff sits at the western edge of one segment of the Delta region, which had been characterized by plantation agriculture and which, consequently, had large numbers of minority poor. Another reason governing the decision to locate the Good Faith Fund there was also some notion that the fund should operate on its own, free from an identification with the Elk Horn Bank.

There is something attractive to the general public, at least to its media representatives, about an organization like the Good Faith Fund. There is charm in the idea that the model is borrowed from a third world country. There is an appeal about low-income people pulling themselves up by their bootstraps and doing so within a capitalist and entrepreneurial tradition. It represents the move from dependence on the welfare state to a sturdy independence. And the idea of lending money to the poor is novel. Finally, the narrative of a group of low-income people coming together to give each other advice and support as they embark on the entrepreneurial venture makes a good story. The enterprising borrowers, with their tough pride, made good copy as they did not fit stereotypes of either business people or standard ideas about the poor.

Because of this, the Good Faith Fund was the object of much publicity. Its managers appeared on national television and its story was written in the national press. Documentary filmmakers wanted to include the enterprise in their films on economic development strategies.

The irony was that the division with the smallest budget and possibly with the least early successes came, in the minds of many outsiders, to stand for the whole organization. This was a source of frustration to the managers and workers of other divisions within Southern.

Building the Initial Staff

Much of the top management of the company was recruited after an extensive national search. Each of them brought an impressive record with them, and, indeed, they were impressive people. In their new jobs, however, none of them was doing precisely what he or she had ever done before. The head of Opportunity Lands was a graduate of Yale's School of Management and, for some time, a member of the administrative team of one of the country's best-known and most charismatic mayors. A Stanford Business School MBA who had been involved in not-for-profit activity in California, but who ultimately became a plant manager for a Fortune 500, Midwestern manufacturer, became the leader of AEG. A Massachusetts Institute of Technology graduate with a Master's degree in urban planning, also a native of California, who had been working for Shorebank in Chicago, moved to Pine Bluff to create the Good Faith Fund. Also in the group that went initially to staff the new company were a graduate of the Yale School of Management who had worked for Shorebank in Chicago and a Dartmouth graduate and Arkansas native who had also worked in Chicago. The only person in the group who was not a graduate of a northern elite university was the president of Southern Ventures, a native of Minnesota, who came to Southern with a reputation as a tough manager and who had helped to save an economically development-oriented manufacturing organization with several businesses in Mississippi.

The only manager whose job represented a clear continuity from the past was the man who had been president of the Elk Horn Bank under the old management and who initially stayed on to run the bank. However, the newcomers' plans made him uneasy. He had taken over the bank when its former owner had been in serious trouble, and he was nervous about "development loans," which he translated as weak loans. He was uneasy about using Small Business Administration guarantees to buttress loans because he believed a good loan should not need any help, and he was nervous that the service area the new company had in mind was too large to be adequately monitored. Consequently, he quickly found a new position, and he left to take over a bank in his wife's nearby hometown. This manager had been the only southerner, to say nothing of the only Arkansan, in the company's top management—a point worth noting.

In many parts of the United States, the fact that people hired by an organization are not local would hardly be noted. It is difficult to imagine someone asking Shorebank, for example, how many of its employees or managers were Illinoisians or even Midwesterners. Similarly, one would be unlikely to ask how many faculty members at the University of Chicago are from Chicago. However, when one moves to Arkansas, particularly rural Arkansas, one encounters two levels of regional self-consciousness unusual for much of the rest of the United States. The first of these levels relates to the American South. The second relates specifically to Arkansas. As John Shelton Reed (1983) points out, the South is such a distinctive region with a strong sense of collective identity that its residents might be considered members of an ethnic group. Given the amount of mobility between North and South, one could make too much of this. Nonetheless, coupled to distinctive tastes in food and a distinctive way of speaking, southerners also display a shared consciousness. This is heightened in rural areas, where there has been less migration from the North than in the major cities. There is a vast literature on the distinctiveness of the South, and this is not the place to review it. But the issue of being a southerner or an Arkansan is particularly important to note for the purposes of this account. One of the South's distinctions compared to the rest of the United States is a commitment to localism and place. Southerners, compared to northerners, are less likely to go far from home for college, for example. When asked to identify personal heroes, they are much more likely to mention family members as compared to well-known public figures (Reed 1983).

Arkansans share the general southern viewpoint, but, in addition, there is something about Arkansas history that exaggerates both localism and wariness toward "outsiders." There seems to be in Arkansas a collective sense of inferiority, not only in relationship to the North, but to the other states of the South as well. I have already mentioned that, in their efforts to buy a bank, Shorebank managers encountered resistance as outsiders. With an organization like Southern, whose origins are in Chicago, one was likely to hear talk about carpetbaggers. Arkansans believe that northerners and maybe much of the rest of the country view them with condescension. When I was exploring prospects of observing Southern in action for this research project, the head of a local foundation tried to discourage me, explaining that northerners did not understand or respect southerners and that urban people considered rural people inferior. Therefore, my capacity to analyze with impartial understanding would be unlikely.

At the time of President Clinton's election in 1992, there was much comment in the newspapers and talk on the street about how the state would now have a newly positive image after the embarrassment over the integration of Central High School and the role of Governor Orville Faubus, despite the fact that this event took place as long ago as 1957. After Clinton's election, a number of people reported in elated casual conversation, "Now Arkansas has something positive to show the world." Part of the rage many Arkansans have since expressed about President Clinton's subsequent personal behavior comes from the belief that the state was publicly humiliated once again. Several people I interviewed also cited, without my asking, a female television character who was quoted as saying, "I don't know anything. I'm just from Arkansas. I just watch television and do my hair." In another example of cultural stereotypes, the song "Two Little Girls from Little Rock," from the 1953 movie *Gentlemen Prefer Blondes*, explains how good-looking country bumpkins, following a well-established path, use their obvious physical attributes to get what they want from men. Indeed, it is true that one can find other perceived aspects of Arkansas life that are repeated as national jokes. The point here is that many Arkansas residents are suspicious of northerners, whom they think are condescending, and they will often close down when dealing with them.

The Central High School crisis is obviously a symbol of historical racial prejudice. Many southerners believe (perhaps correctly) that northerners assume that southerners still harbor particularly intense racial prejudice. I was continually astonished during my first months in Arkansas by the number of people who took me aside to explain that they were not prejudiced, although I had not raised the subject. It was clear that they expected Yankees to think that they were. As evidence for their lack of prejudice, they often told stories of old African American family servants who were, they said, treated as family members, or about black friends they had had during military experience.

So, to the extent that Shorebank was a Chicago company and almost all of the early highly ranked and visible Southern officials were northerners or "Yankees," some resentment and suspicion in the community was generated. This despite the fact that the Southern managers came to Arkadelphia from all over the United States because they were positively motivated by Southern's mission. In addition, around Arkadelphia, the word was out that almost all of these new people came from elite East Coast and West Coast colleges and universities. That distinction added something to the locals' feelings of being somehow declassed, as well as making the other employees of the Southern subsidiaries feel that, without elite college resumes, there were limits to their promotion opportunities. These feelings were compounded by the implicit message from Southern: "We are going to end the poverty in which you people are mired, just like a third world country."

Although not having more visible Arkansans in the program may look like another of those early decisions that shaped the future and represented misjudgment as well, it is easy to see why local recruitment was not perceived as a problem by the Chicago management team. They set out on a national search to find the best people they could. The group they came up with had very impressive credentials. It might almost seem self-evident that finding the best people available would be the best way to ensure success. In addition, one diagnosis about the economic problems of the South could lead to the conclusion that outsiders would be the best agents of change.

If part of the diagnosis of the problem is either that traditional forms of behavior—in this case, banking—are blocking progress or that local leaders are holding people down to perpetuate their own interests—and both of these were in the Shorebank diagnosis—one might want outsiders in the job who do not have traditional commitments either to historic patterns of behavior or to traditional power relations.

It should be added that, after the first Elk Horn Bank president resigned, an intense effort to find a new president from Arkansas failed when some of the best candidates communicated that they did not want to live in the small town of Arkadelphia. Ironically, when management finally chose the new president, an officer of the Shorebank Company in Chicago and a University of Chicago graduate, many local people believed that the choice was foreordained and that the search to find an Arkansan for the job was a charade. What is clear is that the paucity of visible southerners, much less Arkansans, worked against a smooth and well-supported start-up and continued to be a problem.

This particular problem was compounded by the attention that attended Southern's arrival. Having made very large financial commitments, local backers were eager to assert that this group of outsiders had the answer to Arkansas's economic problems. They could end poverty, and, although it was only implicit, the assumption was that they knew how to do it a lot better than local people. This publicity both raised expectations unreasonably, on the one hand, and aroused resentment among those who had worked on development in the past, on the other. There were two development agencies in Arkadelphia at the time: a state-funded economic development center at Henderson State University and a small business development center funded by the Small Business Administration. Southern—not without justification—displayed little interest in working with either. In addition, the business school at Henderson State University offered to provide an entrepreneurship training course to assist Southern in its efforts. The offer was not accepted. In all cases, there may have been good reasons not to take these up—for example, one of the first deals brought to the Elk Horn Bank by one of the agencies involved a convicted felon who did not have prior experience in the business he wished to create. Nonetheless, coupled with all of the foregoing, the clear lack of interest in cooperation had the consequence of arousing resentment and creating an unhelpful atmosphere.

The other problem with using outsiders is that, by definition, they lack local knowledge that may be important in making business judgments. Let me put this in perspective. The first Elk Horn Bank president so valued on-the-ground knowledge about what was going on that he did not really want his bank making loans outside of Clark County, despite the fact that Southern's mission was to energize all of south Arkansas. He thought that, to be an effective banker, it was important to know a great deal already about the potential borrower's character, the person's history, and something about the business in which the person was involved. In the service of that kind of knowledge, he liked driving by the businesses of his borrowers to look for signs, such as empty employee parking lots, which would indicate that things were not going as well as the borrower had reported to his loan officer. One should be careful about the effectiveness of such strategies. For they may be reports about ritual behavior to reduce uncertainty, reports which, in fact, do not have much basis in reality. Again, local bankers may have long-term prejudices against people who are unable to live down an unjustly formed reputation. And, of course, being local does not guarantee that one knows what is going on. One very visible and superficially successful contractor in town astonished everybody, including his long-term local resident loan officer, by, one day, without notice, closing his doors and declaring bankruptcy.

Still, the contrast between the level of local knowledge of this local banker and the position of people arriving from out of town is stark. How could the new people make adequate judgments about who is to be trusted? Even if the new members of the management team had been experienced bankers and economic development practitioners, they might have approached this new setting with a certain amount of insecurity. After Southern was in business, many people approached them with offers of assistance, with business deals, and, in some cases, with warnings. If one does not have a good feel for the local terrain, whom does one believe?

One early set of negotiations illustrates the problem. One of the first business proposals made to Southern concerned a local African American businesswoman who had developed a substantial reputation as a dressmaker. Among other things, she had designed an inaugural gown for Hillary Clinton. She was closely connected to a successful local businessman who was the head of the Clark County Industrial Council—a local volunteer group interested in promoting development—and an important local political ally of the Clintons. In fact, he subsequently became a state senator.

Initially, she wanted to start a clothing-manufacturing business specializing in producing military uniforms. She believed she would have an advantage doing this because, as a minority entrepreneur, she would have access to contract set-asides created for the purpose of encouraging minority entrepreneurship. She also had available to her a number of experienced seamstresses who had lost their jobs when Levi Strauss closed a local plant. She was brought to Southern's attention by the local Small Business Development officer who had worked with her on her business plan.

Despite the fact that she had even appeared in a Shorebank-produced video as an example of local entrepreneurship, she was rejected for the loan. Explanations were that she did not have manufacturing experience and that the seamstresses knew how to make pants but did not know how to make shirts. At a subsequent time, she did get a loan from AEG. But, in a single stroke and for a small amount of money, fifteen thousand dollars, the Southern management antagonized her, the best-connected political figure in town who was also interested in development, and the head of the Small Business Development Center.

Although she never did produce uniforms for the military, she is still in business today manufacturing hospital clothing and school uniforms, as well as continuing her original dressmaking and tailoring operation. In a world where personal ties and networks and the construction of networks of relationships are important, insecure outsiders made a serious misjudgment. In my own travels through the community, I subsequently heard cries of rage about this case from both the political figure and the Small Business Development officer. The woman herself, despite having subsequent dealings with Southern, never became one of its fans. With better ties to the community, this misjudgment would not have taken place. What made this matter more serious is that one of Southern's missions was to improve the plight of African Americans. Through the first five years of the company's life, with the exception of micro-loans made through the Good Faith Fund, it made very few loans to minority entrepreneurs.

CHAPTER 3

Beginnings

There is a vague and ill-defined quality which, unacknowledged and often poorly understood, represents a fundamental prize in organizational controversy. This is the evolving character of the organization as a whole. What are we? What shall we become? With whom shall we be identified? What are our roots? . . . To reflect upon such long-run implications is to seek the indirect consequences of day-to-day behavior for those fundamental ideals and commitments which serve as a foundation for loyalty and effort.

—PHILIP SELZNICK, *TVA and the Grass Roots*

As Selznick suggests, beginnings are peculiarly important because what happens at the start lays out a trajectory that helps to shape the future. As things are set in motion, patterns are established that, once underway, are hard to alter. Max Weber compares that process to a set of dice loaded in such a way that, with each throw, the probability increases that a particular pattern will reappear. The Chicago team faced the problem of getting started with special intensity because Southern Development Bancorporation was locally acephalous.

Confronted by the fact that, with the exception of one manager, who, unfortunately, had no prior management experience, none of the managers hired to work in Arkansas had worked for Shorebank in Chicago, and concerned about communicating a distinctive corporate ethos, Shorebank's top management decided to guide the company from Chicago, with a demanding schedule of weekly or biweekly trips to Arkansas to supervise activities there while continuing with their Chicago duties. Shorebank management believed that, although there were some tools available that could be mastered in doing development, real development skills could not be codified but instead grew from a culture and a set of orientations that could only be learned in a hands-on fashion.

These Shorebank managers themselves operated in Arkansas with a handicap. Although people of great talent and ability, they were not able to contribute local knowledge, nor did they have the time to build the kind of local ties that promote acceptance. As important people, they were respected. But it was with wary respect, since they were, after all, outsiders. In the world of a small southern town, as I have suggested before, the outsider issue was not a trivial one.

But the Chicagoans believed that their presence was essential to communicate the distinctive Shorebank culture and the way the company approached the development process. They thought their approach was difficult to learn outside of the context of experience. There are three reasons for this. The first is that the development process is not standardized; there is no manual with a set of procedures to turn to, and each approach must be sensitive to distinctive local conditions. Under those circumstances, underlying value commitments and orientations are more important than rules.

Secondly, Shorebank was an unusual organization. There are few organizations devoted to the twin goals of doing development, on the one hand, and also making a profit, on the other. Most community development organizations are not-for-profits, and often those involved in that world look at for-profit organizations with some skepticism. By contrast, those in for-profit organizations tend to view those who want to "do good" as wasting resources and not being rigorous or serious. The Shorebank model required achieving development in a way that made business sense. All employees, then, had to walk a difficult line—and one that had to be understood almost intuitively. People with good business skills tend to downplay development activities that may reduce profitability. People who want to do good tend not to think about rates of return. In some cases, they think of profit-makers as corrupt.

Third, because most of the funds for Shorebank came from the not-for-profit, foundation-oriented world, one had to learn how to keep the representatives of those foundations satisfied that the company was carrying out its mission, and one had to be alert to opportunities to attract new funds. The task of Shorebank management, then, was to create a distinctive ethos instead of just teaching people how to use a set of tools. This appeared particularly important to do in this case, not only because the management of Southern was disconnected from Shorebank, but because it had little experience doing development at all.

This lack of experienced new managers, coupled with their strong respect for their own capacities, created its own set of problems. If local managers doubted their own capacities to achieve development goals, they demonstrated little apparent evidence.

Consequently, the local managers began to resent the regular arrivals of their Chicago bosses—or were they consultants? Their attitude represents the almost classic story of frontline troops who do not believe that the more distant officers can understand their problems. After all, Arkadelphia and Pine Bluff were not Chicago. In this case, their disapproval was compounded by their recognition of the fact that commuting from Chicago to Arkadelphia costs money. Local managers felt thinly capitalized given the tasks they were to achieve, and they thought the added value that they received from Chicago did not compensate for the costs of getting it. Payments to Shorebank for travel and time came to be called "the money burn." Local managers came to feel that their approaches were the correct ones, and they often did not accept the management philosophy that the Chicago top managers were propounding. The director of the venture capital company felt heavily constrained by what he considered the banker's anti-risk ideology. He followed the model of venture capitalists described above, where issues such as collateral were not high on the list of prerequisites for investment, and where, in the pursuit of large returns, one places substantial resources at risk based on the business model and the quality of management. In the venture capital world, three out of five investments might fail, a fourth might move along unspectacularly, and a fifth would provide rich returns. No bank could operate with such a batting average. But, for the venture capitalist, profits come as the company grows and succeeds or becomes a takeover target of a larger company. His model saw the economy of the region in such serious trouble that it took big risks and big investments to alter the local business terrain. From his perspective, the bank model was timid and inadequate to the size and scope of the problem.

In that spirit, credit, and the resulting debt it engendered, was not a good development instrument. Companies faced with substantial debt service would not be able to ratchet themselves up in a meaningful way, because they were not making the best use of all their resources.

AEG's manager, on the other hand, thought the company did not operate in enough of a business-like fashion. Coming from the industrial world, he expected tighter financial controls, clearer reporting procedures, and more discipline in the way Southern was operating. In addition, because AEG as a not-for-profit had to be chartered as a separate company, he did not always see himself as part of Southern and therefore was not constrained by Southern's procedures and rules. Alarmed by his inadequate funding, he thought he was being pushed into activity that did not make economic sense while, in his judgment, foundation funds would not be forthcoming to support some of the ambitious plans.

The first director of the Opportunity Lands Corporation quit during the first year. Also struggling with ambitious plans and thin funding, she had few resources left after the completion of her first excellent project. Her replacement was the only native Arkansan in the top team. At one point, she had been an important housing official for the state of Arkansas. She understood herself to be the only carrier of local knowledge, local mores, and the only one with a sense of how the state bureaucracy worked.

The director of the Good Faith Fund, coming from Chicago, felt that she had a special understanding of how the Shorebank team conducted business. Besides, she was working with an operational model from Bangladesh. She also chose to go her own way.

The result of all this is that nobody captured the organization's soul in the way that Selznick describes. More than that, during the recruiting process, some of the new managers came to believe that, after Shorebank created Southern and set it running, its management was supposed to withdraw. Given the lack of shared values and the concern with the expenditure of funds that Shorebank's management required for its travels, the Southern team was eager for Shorebank to disconnect from the process. At one point, they wrote a letter to the Shorebank management asking them for a schedule of their plan to relinquish power. As might be guessed, that memo did not improve ties between the local group and Chicago management. Ultimately, unable to find an Elk Horn Bank president in Arkansas, Shorebank did send to Arkadelphia one of its vice presidents both to operate the Elk Horn Bank and to be CEO of the whole Southern operation. But the other managers, already in place with operating companies, never fully accepted his authority.

The point is, then, that nobody won over or defined the organization's soul from the beginning, and, as an organization, it never moved in a clear direction, with managers tussling with each other and their Chicago "bosses."

As one might guess, mangers also did not work well together. At one point, an outsider who was reading the strategic plan asked if these were separate companies or a coordinated unit. Early in the process, top management in Chicago had some notion that excessive cooperation among the group in Arkansas inhibited entrepreneurial energy and became an excuse for not succeeding. That orientation changed over time. So much so that, several years later, Southern hired a consultant/coach whose job it was, through retreats and strategic planning efforts, to build a more focused and integrated organization. It is not clear what the consequences of her effort were. Subsequent events suggest that they bore little fruit.

Other Entry Issues

The fight for the organization's soul as discussed by Selznick has two elements. On the one hand is the issue of internal activity that we have just discussed. The other is the message that the company sends to its potential allies and constituents, and how it comes to be perceived.

The first one, then, is about defining the goals and purposes of an organization and the methods it will use to achieve them. These definitions become guides in the course of the decision-making process. They may be implicit or explicit, but they are the stars by which one steers. As we have seen, no one really gained control of the organization's culture and central direction. This direction was determined, in many respects, by congeries of different agendas.

The second aspect, how the organization looks to the outside world, may or may not be a different story. But it, too, helps to shape what the organization becomes, for the organization is in interaction with its environment, and how that environment responds will have serious internal consequences. On the one hand, what messages does the organization send as it enters the community? And, on the other, how are these messages perceived? Those two questions may become more alike over time, as people come to understand the organization better. But they may also grow further apart. Wittingly or unwittingly, an organization sends out messages to multiple audiences—supporters, clients, and individuals in the surrounding community. Some of these messages are explicit and some are symbolic. Some arise from observed behavior and others may be understood differently by the senders and by the recipients. How they are shaped and organized will become an important element in determining the relationship to the community.

That relationship is important to the success or failure of the organization. This is one of those matters that may seem obvious, but needs to be underscored. One cannot just hang out a sign and say "Here we are" and expect clients to come marching to the door. They will instead come through a network of referrals built through an array of contacts. And who comes will depend on how the organization is perceived, as well as the nature of the networks through which the information travels. Clients are only one part of the process. In order to fight a war on poverty, one needs allies. The development process in southern Arkansas, operating over twenty-one thousand square miles in which some 650,000 people resided, was not something to be achieved by simply spending $12 million. To be successful, one needed to build coalitions that would march in the same direction and to establish local relationships with committed people who would help generate shared and multi-pronged efforts.

To understand the Southern story fully, it is necessary to describe something about the origins of Shorebank. (For more detailed information see Taub 1988.) As outlined in chapter 1, Shorebank in Chicago began as a grossly undercapitalized company with the goal of investing in an inner-city community, Chicago's South Shore, through the purchase of a bank (the South Shore Bank) in order to halt that community's decline. To get its start, the founding group used $800,000 and additional borrowed funds to purchase a bank which had fewer than $40 million in assets. The bank itself was in decline through deliberate mismanagement: depositors were leaving, and the bank's owners, hoping to move the bank's charter, were not reinvesting to upgrade or even maintain the existing operation. The whole enterprise, then, began as a struggle with a very small operation, and in a small corner of Chicago. Outside of a small circle of investors and friends, nobody knew it existed.

In terms of its visibility through its early years, one might think of the South Shore Bank as a stealth entry. Company employees were able to work outside the spotlight, straightening out the bank, developing their tools, building relationships in the community, and taking the time to understand the community in which they worked. Following a common, local political model, the early founders attended a series of neighborhood coffee meetings arranged for them by local people, and they made the rounds of other places where people gather, such as churches. It should be added that South Shore was not an exotic and distant locale. One of the founders actually lived in South Shore, and two of the others lived in adjacent communities.

By contrast, Southern entered Arkansas in a much more visible but, at the same time, less grassroots-oriented way. Because of the success of its progenitors in Chicago, it was supported by prominent national foundations—the Ford Foundation in New York and the MacArthur Foundation in Chicago. Initially invited to Arkansas by Governor Clinton, it was also supported by the state's two largest foundations. As I have discussed, its board consisted of some of the most important people in the state. Unlike the Shorebank situation, this was not a stealth entry. Some of the board members had personal reasons for calling attention to the operation, thus raising expectations and misunderstandings.

One can begin to see outlines of what this operation looked like to residents of Arkadelphia, the main locale in which the company was visible. From the local perspective, a large organization with substantial resources, whose staff consisted primarily of Yankees, had arrived in town with some kind of mandate to "do good." But it was hard to escape the perception that these outsiders were doing pretty well for themselves, as well. It was not long before some people in the community began to perceive them as modern-day carpetbaggers, coming to make money to bring back to the North.

Six or seven new people arrived in town with salaries that put them at the high end of Arkadelphia income levels, and they set up offices in the center of town. Their first step was to renovate office space in a building adjacent to the Elk Horn Bank. With their chic industrial grays, cool off-whites, new, modern furniture, and the latest in computers, fax machines, and photocopiers, the offices were probably among the most coolly elegant spaces in Arkadelphia.

Stylistically, this was not a group with whom the local populace could stop and pass the time of day, which, in a town like Arkadelphia, was an important part of life. That stance encouraged a perception that the new managers were arrogant, an interpretation that was reinforced by other behaviors. For example, Southern seemed loath to take on local partners. The dean of a local business school offered to provide instruction for incipient entrepreneurs, but his offer was rejected. There were two public-sector local offices that had economic development as their primary responsibility. One, in fact, was chartered by the Small Business Administration and had the goal of encouraging small businesses. The efforts of the local agencies received scant attention, despite the fact that they were deeply rooted in the community. The director of one of the local agencies had lived in Clark County all his life, had been a banker, and was married to a local schoolteacher. The other, actually a native of Tennessee, was married to a professor in Henderson's School of Business. One of these local directors had worked on the business plan of the dressmaker discussed in chapter 2, whose application had been rejected. It is not hard to guess how they felt about Southern, and they proceeded to tell anybody who listened. But, to tell the story this way is to place blame for maintaining distance solely on the Southern managers.

From another perspective, in the world they were dealing with and in the way they perceived it, these new managers did not see that they had any other choice. This is a more complicated story than one of outsiders who misunderstood local culture. For example, it was not clear what the School of Business had to offer. What does a business school with only a limited, local reputation have to offer graduates of Stanford, Yale, MIT, and the University of Chicago? And if the local development agencies were so good, why had they not achieved more? More than that, the local agency director was a failed banker who seemed, at that moment, to be hooked on a program to encourage the co-generation of electricity using waste products from lumber mills in which the region abounded. (Actually, this man's fertile brain produced a metal fabricators' cooperative association; and an apprenticeship training program connected to it that, in the right circumstances, might have thrived and become a model for others to follow. He was, in fact, a strong idea man who was somewhat weaker on implementation.) The other was a retired military officer. Did he really know much about starting businesses? He relied for support on the students from Henderson's unaccredited business school.

Constructing local collaboration is a difficult matter, exacerbated when one does not know the players very well. To begin with, if these are true collaborations, much time and energy must be spent making them work. And, since different people have different visions and ideas about how to proceed, there is the danger that working with local organizations will dilute the program down the road, based on what seems to be a well-worked-out vision.

All new projects start with enthusiasm and high hopes. The first victories seem easy, and there are expectations—or, perhaps, hopes—that this is the way things will go. One might ask, If it had been that easy, why had others not already achieved what is a widely shared goal? The answer was that the Shorebank group believed it had a special vision and that that vision was the magical key for opening opportunities that had been closed before. There are dangers with such a conception. The first is to fall into thinking that, because one has the key, one is smarter than those who do not. With this comes a form of wariness, making it harder to cooperate with those around you.

Further, one might be wary of connecting with local groups who are tied into the pre-existing power structure. It may be that their standard way of doing things has encouraged the persistence of poverty and, by so doing, kept themselves in an advantaged position. Efforts at economic development would, then, mainly be programs that served to boost their own economic advantages against others (Molotch and Logan 1987).

There is much history of this in the South. For example, Wright (1986) reports that southern elites deliberately opposed spending money for education, since they feared that an educated labor force would cut into their profits. This is not just a speculation based on out-of-date historical perspectives. There was some evidence of this attitude in Arkadelphia. For example, in an effort to attract branch plants of larger businesses to the area, one local development organization produced a video which emphasized that one of the attractions of the region was how hard local residents were willing to work for very low wages. The video had one supervisor reporting his surprise that he could get such high-quality workers for such low pay. There were also business people in town who were not enthusiastic about economic development programs, for that meant they would be bringing businesses to the community and thereby creating a labor shortage that would, following the law of supply and demand, raise the wages of their own employees, thereby reducing company profits.

The key question was, What were the traditions and resources that kept some groups in power and excluded others? Fear of falling into the pattern of strengthening the position of one particular elite group is heightened if part of the vision about generating new opportunities is perceived to be removing the blinders of others—in this case, bankers—that have been created by ill-formed prejudice. The South Shore Bank in Chicago made its name because its founders understood that racial prejudice had clouded the judgments of bankers and people who make loans, and of realtors and developers who decide where to invest real estate dollars. By making real estate loans to minorities who had been red-lined or rejected by traditional bankers and by succeeding in making a profit, Shorebank demonstrated that some of the refusal by bankers to lend money to minority individuals was caused, at least in part, by prejudice rather than careful business analysis. And they perceived this to be a morally inferior position.

In fact, that perception did not quite represent the reality of Arkadelphia. The city had something of a reputation of being more inclusive of minorities in important ways than some of the surrounding communities, as well as those in the Delta. For example, as I discussed previously, the assistant superintendent of the heavily majority-white school district was an African American man. Blacks sat on the Board of the Industrial Corporation. The businesswoman previously discussed, an African American who had wanted a loan to make military uniforms, worked closely with one of the most important political figures in the community, a man who went on to become a state representative.

Thinking about early messages and defining characteristics, there were two events that inadvertently sent clear messages. The first was a celebration of the company's first year of operation. One has to put the event in the context of Clark County, Arkansas: it is poor, and it is dry. There are no liquor stores or bars except for some private clubs and the VFW. The fanciest restaurant in town was the Fish Net, which served catfish and hush puppies but, of course, no alcohol. The Arkadelphia Country Club, which was exempt from the proscription about selling alcohol, specialized in serving hamburgers along with a bottle of beer. The nearest upscale restaurant in the area was in Hot Springs, thirty-six miles away.

But Southern's first-year party, a white-tablecloth catered event in which wine and beer flowed copiously, was not really aimed at local people. Rather, its audience was the funders and supporters of Southern. Most of the board members were present, as were representatives of the major foundations, key people from the large lumber companies, some bankers, and, of course, Shorebank and Southern executives. It was a joyous and self-congratulatory event with numerous speeches and toasts, and recollections about how these Chicagoans had come to Arkadelphia. There was also a multimedia presentation, which included the stories of the dressmaker (who had not gotten the loan and who, subsequently, requested that she no longer be included in Southern's publicity materials) and of a local meat processor whose experiences will be detailed in a later chapter.

The guests were impressed. One of the celebrity board members reported with pleasure, "We could never had done this by ourselves. This is an amazing operation." He was not, I should add, discussing the party, but the establishment of the Southern Development Bancorporation with its full organization. But he did understand the party as being a culminating event in the first stage of a substantial achievement. Lubricated by abundant alcohol, dazzled by the glitter, but also thrilled by the comprehensive organizational structure and the fine people chosen to staff it, the board and its supporters probably felt better about Southern that night than they would ever feel again.

In short, Southern arrived in south Arkansas as a handmaiden of what a local columnist called "the good suit club," which included many of the important people in the Arkansas business community. And, in contrast to the early days of Shorebank in Chicago, it established itself as an elite institution, although not quite of the Clark County world.

Another defining moment was a full-company retreat at a nearby resort, DeGray Lake. The goal of the retreat was to begin to work on a strategic plan for the company's future. This included an overnight stay and meals (more consistent with middle-level local standards). Like the big party, it too was an event of warm, good feeling, although one sensed a kind of edginess as well. All the people who worked for the new company were invited to participate on an equal footing. This included clerical personnel, as well as top management. What became clear was that some of the lower-level personnel wanted to emphasize the nature of the company's mission as they understood it—that is, to help the disadvantaged, particularly African Americans. Management wanted to develop a business plan and to think of a development strategy, which was not necessarily congruent in a simple way with helping the disadvantaged. From their perspective, systems had to be put in place that made both business and development sense. Overall, there were shared goals, but a lack of perception about the route Southern would have to travel to achieve them. This led to a certain measure of disorganization and confusion, as well as heightened tension. The meeting was, in some respects, so upsetting that one of the initial management team left the company shortly afterward, citing events at the meeting as one of the reasons.

The lesson that management took away from this event was that such large, incorporative meetings were of little value. There was too much talk, a certain amount of confusion, and matters did not move forward. Some felt that, although it was important for top managers to meet on a regular basis, lower-level people, who did not understand the complexities of the situation, just muddied the waters. The result was that the top echelon met regularly and, for several years, excluded others in middle management. There was a cost to this in terms of building esprit de corps. Having tasted participation, people were saddened to lose it. But it may also have been that top management became defined so narrowly that important middle-echelon people more closely at the interface between the company and the surrounding world were excluded from the planning process. They became bitter and, in some cases, withheld initiative. It should be added that, at a later stage, after a longer period of work with the coach/management consultant discussed above, whose assignment was to help the various elements of the company work better together, the middle-level group was invited to have their own separate meetings, to have their deliberations communicated to management, and to play a larger role in the planning process.

The result of all this—the complex issues of management by inexperienced people from afar, the nature of the board, the suspicion of outsiders by local people, and internal organizational difficulties—was that nobody gained control of the organization's soul in either of the two senses that the quote by Selznick suggested was necessary. There was no shared internal definition which could become a guide to conduct. And the message sent to the surrounding community with which the organization had to act was unclear. The hiring of the consultant in the strategic planning process was a belated effort to forge a team that both worked together and had a clear mission—that is, it was a belated effort to create a new organizational soul. It was probably a case of too little, too late.

Furthermore, the message, about the organization's mission and what it had to offer, that Southern wanted to send was not one easily understood by local people. The underlying Southern methodology was to provide credit to people who had been blocked from getting credit before. But this did not mean that Southern wanted to make bad banking deals. What, then, is a good deal? It was true, for example, that Southern was able to use the SBA to provide guarantees for parts of loans, reducing exposure to risk for the lenders. Some bankers in Arkansas expressed the belief that "if one needed an SBA guarantee, then the loan must not be good. If it were, one would not need the external guarantee." How to explain that the company was willing, at least in theory, to make loans that banks had historically avoided because they appeared slightly more risky than traditional loans, with the goal of encouraging a sector which had been cut off previously? The logic of the Small Business Administration was to encourage those loans, with the assumption that some of the avoidance of bank participation in them was based on ill-informed prejudice. How to explain that there is a risk/reward curve and that it was possible to move slightly further along that curve and still make good loans, even if they were more expensive to make because the small business owners, lacking experience, needed more guidance to preparing loan packages? Talk of SBA guarantees had one or two of the old Elk Horn Bank officials recalling the difficulties of the bank under an earlier ownership, and the hardship that had caused for so many. Such tales literally brought tears to their eyes. They were quite certain that they did not want to face that possibility again. For some of them, then, the thing called a development loan was, by definition, a bad loan.

At the other extreme, some community members heard the message as "the bank is willing to make loans to anybody." This seemed a chance to make some money easily. As was the case when Shorebank first opened in Chicago, some people with shallow and shady propositions came forward. On the other hand, one fairly well-informed community member kept insisting that the bank sold itself to the public as the lender of last resort, and they ought to be willing to take any plausible deal—"plausible" being defined by this community member as having a very low threshold of acceptability. Every time Southern or AEG rejected a loan application that this fellow knew about, he would announce loudly that the organization was not keeping to its public commitments. Because of the confused image, local development agencies did, in fact, arrive at Southern's doorstep with deals that were not necessarily very good ones—deals without collateral or no equity commitment from the entrepreneur.

The latter is important because, if a businessperson has nothing of his or her own to lose, it is excessively easy to shrug and walk away from a difficult situation, losing only the corporation's resources, including bank loans. Real commitment and effort require that the failure will have a personal and financial cost. One particularly egregious example of a borrower brought to Southern's attention by an economic development agency was that of a convicted felon and long-time acquaintance who had a plan to manufacture shoes, even though his experience in shoe manufacturing was negligible. Whether this was an example of Southern sending an unclear message or of "good old boys" taking care of each other is uncertain. But, either way, it created a problem for a specialized and unusual development organization.

But it is also true that the kind of hybrid organization that made up Southern had a confusing message. At the first-year celebratory party discussed above, one of the board members asked me what made the chairman of Shorebank "tick." He could not understand how somebody could work so hard and so carefully with the "alleged" primary goal of doing good for others. It was mainly a compliment, but one that was tinged with a slight touch of suspicion. Such suspicion was often attached to assessments of Southern's efforts.

Those first years were hard years for Southern. In terms of outputs, these years produced disappointments for knowledgeable local people, funders, and outside observers as well. Many came to hold the view that, after all the public attention, Elk Horn was just another local bank; and, with the exception of some construction and rehabilitation activities that came from Opportunity Lands, they were unable to see any serious accomplishments in the development direction that distinguished Southern's performance from the performance of other local banks. One well-known development expert complained bitterly that Southern was getting too much publicity and diverting resources from other more worthwhile projects (including his own) when it was just mainly a community bank doing what a good community bank does. A local political figure who had been quite negative about Southern changed his view after some time: "Now that I know what they are supposed to be doing, supporting some deals that are slightly more risky than traditional bank loans, I feel much better about them. They are good citizens, and they do make some hard-to-make loans." Why scaled-down expectations for Southern might have been more appropriate, and why some others felt that there was too much publicity for inadequate achievement, is what I will explore in the next chapter.

CHAPTER 4

Problems with the Diagnosis

In chapter 1, we discussed the importance of the diagnosis of a problem for selecting the means to cure it. Lack of credit availability was a central part of Southern's diagnosis. Implicit in that assumption is that people would flock to a source of finance once it was made available without old-fashioned, hide-bound restrictions or prejudice. Reality presented a different face. During those early years, it seemed very difficult to find or make a development loan. In fact, loan volume was a continuing, nagging challenge for all of Southern's divisions. One would have thought that the lack of lending opportunities would have raised questions about the diagnosis, at least in its simplest form. The main result, however, was to encourage management to look harder and to cast its net over a wider territory. In some sense, the story of all the companies, with the exception of Opportunity Lands, is the story of a search for businesses that would benefit from finance. Even Opportunity Lands began by assuming it would be providing business subsidies in the sense of constructing incubators for promising fledglings. It either could not find companies that would benefit from incubators or, in a depressed economy, appropriate business space was so cheap that such subsidies were unnecessary. It, too, found few such opportunities and became, instead, primarily a subsidized housing development organization. The story is not dissimilar from a famous study by Festinger of an organization that predicted the end of the world by a certain date. When the world did not end on that date, instead of collapsing, the organization began to work harder at finding new recruits. In Southern's case, the failure of promising borrowers to materialize led to renewed efforts to find borrowers, rather than to suggestions that maybe credit by itself was not as essential as first imagined.

Obviously, things are not quite as simple as that. People first have to learn that the credit is available. They have to be sure that the providers are legal and that they are not part of some system of exploitation. The lenders have to be people that others would trust with personal financial information. Borrowers need to be able to understand the program. And it might be helpful for them to know that the financing program is appropriate for them.

Southern had problems on all of those counts. Although Southern opened its doors with some fanfare, most people in the targeted areas never came to know about its programs. There was, in fact, no consistent effort to disseminate information. Our survey data show that only a very small proportion of the population in any of the towns where Southern affiliates were most active knew very much about the companies.

See table 4.1, with answers in response to the question, Have you heard of . . . ? We include answers to the question about a government agency with a development agenda, the Arkansas Industrial Development Commission (AIDC), as a point of comparison. We would not expect the same level of recognition for the Southern companies that we would for AIDC, which had been around for a long time and invested millions of dollars annually. But it does provide some evidence of the range of possibilities.

These data have to be looked at with a grain of salt. People are more likely to answer "yes" to questions like these because they do not want to look ignorant. And, in addition, some of the names are confusing or look similar to others. What we can see is that, not surprisingly, the Southern

TABLE 4.1: PERCENTAGE ANSWERING YES TO, HAVE YOU HEARD OF . . . ? IN SELECT ARKANSAS TOWNS					
COMPANY	AIDC	SOUTHERN VENTURES	AEG	GOOD FAITH FUND	OPPORTUNITY LANDS
Town					
Arkadelphia (%)	54.1	10.3	15.1	15.8	11.6
Malvern (%)	49.6	2.3	13.7	10.7	4.6
Pine Bluff (%)	9.6	1.9	1.9	27.6	2.6
Hope (%)	53.5	1.4	11.3	7.0	4.2

divisions were better known in Arkadelphia than they were in the other towns. This makes sense because Arkadelphia was the headquarters town, and, as I have suggested, those who had come to set up business there were quite visible. Similarly, we can see that the Good Faith Fund was very much better known in Pine Bluff than in the other towns. Again, this makes sense because the Pine Bluff region is where the Good Faith Fund operated exclusively. Pine Bluff is a large town with approximately sixty-five thousand people. In such a setting, the arrival of a small group did not have the same visibility as it would have had in Arkadelphia. Under the circumstances, the Good Faith Fund effort represented the one substantial communications achievement of the Southern operation. The one surprising result in table 4.1 was the low level of AIDC recognition in Pine Bluff compared to the other communities. I have no explanation for that. We carried out this survey in seven towns. The average figure for AIDC name recognition was slightly more than a third.

Rather strikingly, according to our surveys of borrowers from the various Southern subsidiaries, even those who received loans from Southern usually learned of their availability by accident—that is, by word of mouth. This was true even in the small town of Arkadelphia.

One satisfied borrower, a well-educated, second-generation, small businessman located in Arkadelphia—the kind of person who was fairly well connected and who should have been the most likely to learn about Southern's efforts—reported that he only learned there were possible loans for him while watching a school soccer game with one of the Elk Horn Bank employees. During a casual discussion about the man's business, he learned from the banker that Elk Horn had loans available that might help him. He was grateful, and one of the few borrowers who expressed great and unambiguous admiration for the Southern program.

With the exception of the Good Faith Fund, where part of the program consisted of loan representatives getting out into the community, there was not very much effort by Southern's other affiliated companies to make their presence known. No adequate advertising campaign was conducted, nor was there a continued and distinctive effort to make contact with accountants and lawyers who might have made referrals.

At a later stage, AMS ran advertisements announcing that it was there to make loans to small businesses. Inquiries appeared at that point, but they were often from outside the targeted areas.

Throughout the state there was a group of officials, affiliated with the Small Business Administration, who operated small business development centers. They gave lectures about taxes and other matters to those with small businesses or those thinking of doing start-ups. They helped credit seekers prepare business plans, as well, putting them into contact with potential lenders. They certainly had the potential of providing customer referrals. The man posted to Arkadelphia gave up on Southern after his client was rejected. Another, in another part of the state, referred credit applications to Southern companies after they had been turned down by all the banks in his territory. He produced beautiful and compelling business plans. However, the majority of businesses he sent to Elk Horn or AEG ultimately failed. The third SBA official in the area did make a few good referrals.

Even many of those who knew about Southern's efforts were not sure what to make of them. Identified as Chicagoans, the company's managers were seen as outsiders whose motives were not easily understood. It was difficult for many to imagine that a business group would arrive from the North to lend money with the intention of helping local people. This wariness is not completely surprising. The South Shore Bank had a similar problem in its own neighborhood back in Chicago when the new management arrived there in 1973. Although that management group did an aggressive job of selling their bank, people tended not to believe them. "People have come here promising to help us, and what they did was mainly to help themselves," some South Shore residents said in the early days. They wanted to see "actions not words." This problem, in Southern's case, was compounded by the distance traveled and the fact that it involved northerners coming South. There were also issues of trust. Unlike the other subsidiaries, Elk Horn Bank was at least an established institution. Many people who borrowed money from Elk Horn did business with lenders who had been part of the community for many years. Young people starting out went to people who had lent money to their parents. There was comfort and security in doing business with such folks. The other companies were comprised of strangers whom nobody knew. There is an old Chicago expression, "We don't deal with nobody nobody sent." The question is, Who can you trust and who can you believe?

But there may be more to the story of finding lenders. In his generative and important book, *The Functions of the Executive* (1938), Chester Barnard makes the point that an effective communication has to be understood. When Southern was introduced to the world, it was always introduced as a complicated story. There was a bank, a separate small business lender, a venture capital company, a lender to very small borrowers who got together in groups, as well as a real estate development company. Often the story was garbled. It was hard to figure out what it was about.

The Good Faith Fund, with a story that intrigued the press, received most of the attention. At that point, the Good Faith Fund required applicants to take a course before they could be considered for a loan. Confusing the whole enterprise of Southern with the Good Faith Fund, many potential borrowers thought they would have to take a course and join groups before they could get a loan. When President Clinton began to talk about banks "like Southern," there was a flurry of newspaper interest. So powerful was the message of training and borrowing groups that sophisticated newspaper reporters hung up on me when, in response to their request for background information on the Southern story, I told them, "No, one does not have to join a group or take a course to get a loan from the Elk Horn Bank or AEG." They hung up because they thought I had the wrong information. At any rate, there were people out there in the small business world who thought they would have to do something that seemed to them distasteful or onerous before they could get a loan, or that the loans available were either too small or too big.

The message to potential borrowers was made even more complicated in practice. Both Southern Ventures and AEG agreed that they did not want to lend to or invest money in retail businesses, because they believed that such companies did not generate economic growth. Instead, they preferred to find either "import substituting" manufacturers, people who could produce goods in Arkansas that currently were being imported from other states, or manufacturers to produce new products that would cause economic growth. One of the companies also developed a complex loan/investment package that was intelligently conceived, but very difficult to explain. I will discuss that program below.

Connected to the question of what the loans were and who they were for was a larger picture of intended targets. In this case, either because of the emphasis on economic development or because the Good Faith Fund, which got most of the attention, heavily targeted African Americans (all of its "poster children" in the company's promotion campaign were black), many people came to believe Southern's program was for black people only. This did not lead to a stampede on the company by African Americans, but it did cause some whites to stay away. After Southern had been in business for eight years, I met an elderly lawyer in one of the Delta communities who reported proudly about how he had helped to keep "that black people's bank" out of town.

In summary, then, there never was a stampede of people trying to get loans or investments from Southern. One could argue that this meant that the diagnosis was wrong—that, indeed, there were not large numbers of credit-starved people. But one can also explain that lack of stampede by the fact that Southern never did become well known or, if it did, that its message was not clear. To the extent that it was known, it was not trusted, its programs were too complicated to be easily understood, and they were believed to be targeted exclusively to a minority population.

Before turning to efforts to generate volume, let me turn to some other issues of strategy.

Target: Southern Arkansas

Capitalized at $12 million, the Southern Development Bancorporation was created to "transform the economy of Southern Arkansas," an area of twenty-seven counties, spread over twenty-one thousand square miles, with a population of about 650,000. And it was to do that by finding entrepreneurs and encouraging them to grow businesses. Given the number of dollars and the size of the staff, the focus on such a large area was not a viable strategy. Shorebank's success had taken place in the South Shore community, an area very much smaller—not much larger than a square mile—with an incredibly dense population of 75,000 residents. Clearly, in Southern's case, a decision had to be made to focus on something smaller and more manageable than the entire southern section of the state.

Among the possible focusing strategies one might use to grow an economy in a region using credit tools, two choices faced Southern. The first is place-related or territorial, and it closely represents the way Shorebank went about its business in Chicago. There, the company targeted one community, South Shore, and focused on it, concentrating its resources and efforts on that area. Using that approach, one expects that the density and volume of activity will create a kind of synergy in which some activities feed off of others and multiply outcomes beyond the size of the original investment. For example, a concentration of real estate renovation will increase the attractiveness of the area, making it a target for other investors and maybe lenders as well. By contrast, a dispersed effort in fixing up a building here and then another five miles away will probably not have consequences beyond the improved property itself. In addition, when work takes place within a concentrated area, renovators can share with each other; what they learn makes them more efficient at their tasks while, at the same time, providing jobs for people with tradesmen's skills. If an area then gets the reputation of being a coming place, it attracts all kinds of market interest. This was the approach favored by Shorebank management.

Another choice of strategy might be to focus on those regional economic sectors that have already shown some vitality or have some kind of market advantage, rather than to restrict oneself to narrowly defined territories. There may be abundant raw materials, cheap transportation, a cadre of trained workers, or access to distinctive markets.

For example, the poultry industry succeeded in Arkansas because there was a vast quantity of underutilized, low-cost land, and farmers who wanted to hold onto it. Two or three large chicken houses could pay the rent and make a little profit. In addition, the climate is moderate, and transportation costs are low for supplying the grain. Arkansas now has expertise, as well, in grain production and distribution to feed the chickens, and the array of equipment—from incubators to automated feeders—to grow them quickly and economically. There is a great effort, as well, to develop new kinds of "value added" poultry products.

In southwestern Arkansas, farmers raise cattle—mainly calves to be sold to grazers in other states, who would then send the grown cattle to feedlot operators prior to slaughter. Perhaps there might be a way to innovate in livestock production, which would bring more money into the region.

We will see that Southern dabbled in a sectoral approach. But it is also true that some of the particular sectors I am describing were unlikely to bring real wealth to an area. Another possible sector with development promise connected to the timber industry. Two-thirds of Arkansas is covered by forest, much of it owned by a few paper companies. One might decide to focus, then, on the wood and wood-products sector, supporting companies that had innovative growth strategies. This strategy would require something of a leap. For, as is the case in many low-wage areas around the world, extractive industries, such as timber, do not provide a firm basis for growth and, in fact, are historically associated with exploitation.

Since the Chicago strategy for development had been place related, and it was the way that the Chicago team thought about the process of doing development, the general goal of the company was to be defined in a place-related way. The problem, then, was to find the correct places to target. One was looking, however, at a whole region that was poorer than the state average and in many cases had very low population densities.

Table 4.2 gives a summary of the income figures. I have included Washington County because that is the center of prosperity in the northwestern section of the state that I alluded to in chapter 1.

Clearly, Arkadelphia and Clark County had to be one of the project's targets. It was the home of Southern's Elk Horn Bank and the company

TABLE 4.2: SELECTED STATISTICS FOR THE STATE OF ARKANSAS, SOUTHERN ARKANSAS COUNTIES, AND WASHINGTON COUNTY (NORTHWESTERN ARKANSAS)

	POPULATION	% OF WHITE	MEDIAN HOUSEHOLD INCOME	PER CAPITA INCOME	% OF POOR
Arkansas	2,673,400	80.00	$32,182	$16,904	15.80
Southern counties	650,464	68.93	$28,729	$15,056	19.65
Washington County	34,691	88.00	$34,691	$17,341	14.60

headquarters, as well. From the perspective of the earlier bank employees and its owner, as well as some others in the community, it seemed that rather than having Clark County be one of a series of targets, maybe it should be the only target. In fact, as I have discussed before, the president of the bank was leery of extending the reach of lending activity beyond the county's boundaries. There were three reasons he thought that lending activity should be close to home. It should be added that, with all the publicity associated with Southern coming to town, many of Clark County's community leaders expected that their home county would be the entire target of the development activity. Whatever the case, Clark County was home base and had to be in the target area. Indeed, the high unemployment rate in the low teens, generated by plant closings, was one of the rationales for locating there. But also, with its two universities, attractive neighborhoods, and a newly constructed industrial park, Arkadelphia, which was also the county seat, appeared to be a good base of activity and an attractive place in which to work.

Criteria varied somewhat in picking the other places to target. At the beginning, the company was looking for towns that were severely impacted, had good labor forces, and had displayed a kind of enlightened leadership. This last point meant that they were places where the white leaders were accustomed to working with the minority community and prepared to open up opportunities to its members. Arkadelphia, for example, certainly seemed to be that sort of place. I have already mentioned the assistant school superintendent and the fact that the local industrial development council included African Americans among its membership. After an incident involving minority students at Henderson State University, which had a growing African American presence, its president also made it clear in a dramatic way that discrimination of any sort would not be tolerated on the campus.

However, another choice constraint began to loom large: How long would it take to get places from Arkadelphia? One might know in the abstract that the population was spread out, and that much transportation took place on rural two-lane roads. In almost an echo of the Elk Horn Bank president's reservations, the new managers were already feeling the limitations about how much could be accomplished in a day, as they spent hours in the company cars driving from place to place. What emerged from the selection process, initially, was that the four nearest big towns were selected as targets (all with populations of ten thousand people or more), with some additional interest in Pine Bluff, which was the home of the Good Faith Fund, and possibly a future point of entry into the Delta.

The towns selected included Malvern, Camden, and Hot Springs. Malvern was demographically very similar to Arkadelphia, without the two colleges. Located about thirty miles northeast, its population had been very dependent on Reynolds Aluminum for employment, and Reynolds's closing had a profound impact. Like Arkadelphia, it was also a county seat, in this case of Hot Spring County. Its nondescript downtown consisted mainly of vacant storefronts. Whatever real business had been located there had since moved to the WalMart, a few miles out of town and along Interstate 30. Unlike Arkadelphia, it displayed severe racial tensions, and one of its suburbs had the fastest-growing school system in the state, a product of white flight. Also, unlike Arkadelphia, Malvern had an absence of community leadership.

Camden dropped out of the picture quite quickly. A town with a population of fifty thousand, it had been an industrial city with a cluster of military contractors located there, including Ling Temco Vought and General Dynamics. It had fallen on hard times as military contracts dried up. Southern staff members could never connect to anyone in that city, and few loans were ever made there.

Hot Springs, which, to confuse everybody, is the seat of Garland County, has since become famous as the place where President Clinton grew up. Hot Springs had been famous as the wide-open sin city of the region; but, even somewhat cleaned up, it still had a slightly raffish character. Unlike Clark and Hot Spring counties, it allowed the public sale of alcohol. Coming into Garland County from either Hot Spring or Clark counties,

FIGURE 4.1: MAP OF SOUTHWEST ARKANSAS

one knew that he or she had crossed the county line because of the immediate presence of liquor stores and bars. It was the place to find topless establishments and street walkers, and it possessed the only race track in the state. At the time of the racing season, all the hotels and motels were filled by horseracing fans from the entire southern region. A complicated city, it had other personalities as well. Its hot springs were an attraction for the elderly; its beautiful old bathhouses and picturesque lakes were magnets for tourists; and it also included a national park that ran right up to its classic old hotels. Some people concerned about economic development had attempted to make it into an attractive place for artists, and during the 1990s several galleries opened in Hot Springs, along with an annual foreign film festival. Submerged somewhat below all the color was a manufacturing city, the home of the Munro Shoe Company, the production of sharpening stones, and some thriving small manufacturers.

Southern also had some investments in nearby Hope. When the project began, Hope was in decline, similar to the conditions in Arkadelphia

TABLE 4.3: ARKANSAS COUNTY DATA

COUNTY (TOWN)	POPULATION	% OF WHITE	MEDIAN HOUSEHOLD INCOME	PER CAPITA INCOME	% OF POOR
Clark (Arkadelphia)	28,845	74.3	$28,845	$14,533	19.1
Garland (Hot Springs)	88,068	88.9	$31,724	$18,631	14.6
Hempstead (Hope)	23,587	63.3	$28,622	$14,103	20.3
Hot Spring (Malvern)	30,353	87.3	$31,543	$15,216	14.0
Jefferson (Pine Bluff)	84,278	48.5	$31,327	$15,417	20.5
Phillips (Helena)	26,445	39.2	$22,231	$12,288	32.7

Note: Clark County probably includes some student incomes. Phillips County includes West Helena, which has somewhat higher incomes.

and Malvern. It did house one nationally known, indeed, internationally known, manufacturer—Klipschorn, renowned for its high-quality speaker systems. However, Hope was also the birthplace of Bill Clinton. When he began his bid for the presidential nomination, the state of Arkansas allotted to Hope increased incentives to attract businesses, and a number of new manufacturers opened there. Many of Hope's working residents commuted to nearby Nashville, the home of Poulin Weed-Eater, a growing national manufacturer, and also the home of a major cutlery producer.

Later in the process, with continuing pressure to do development activity in the Delta, Opportunity Lands, the Good Faith Fund, and AMS all attempted development activity in Helena. Located on the Mississippi, in the heart of the Delta, with a population of approximately eighteen thousand, it was in far more serious straits than any of the other communities under consideration. With a minority population of 60 percent, its unemployment rates were in excess of 20 percent and its poverty rates were even higher. In these respects, it was no better or worse than the other nearby Delta counties. Previous efforts at development in Helena had consisted of trying to revitalize a historic downtown, which had charming early twentieth-century storefronts (most in serious distress); the construction of a market place; the rehabilitation of grand old mansions, some of which were converted to bed and breakfast inns; the construction of a Delta museum, which displayed materials about the history of the region; and attempts to attract resources for the development of the harbor and port. It also attracted tens of thousands of people each autumn to a blues festival. None of these activities seemed to have any impact on the economy of the community.

Economic Development Theory

The idea of doing economic development has a rich history. Although it is true that the South had important economic development programs in the 1930s, most visibly the Tennessee Valley Authority, major national attention to economic development began with the success of the Marshall Plan after the Second World War, and then followed with the application of development efforts to the third world countries—particularly in Africa and Asia, but also Latin America—as they emerged from the colonial experience and became independent nations. In the early years of both thinking about and trying to achieve development, many people brought to the task great enthusiasm that had been generated by the success of the Marshall Plan experience. That confidence was soon destroyed when it turned out that there was no miracle plan for development, as political institutions and politicians, traditional customs, and historic exploitative relations with their former colonial masters all seemed to contrive to undermine efforts at economic growth. The Marshall Plan aimed at *re*building successful economies. Efforts in the third world were aimed at building modern economies, where none had been before. An early important theorist of the development movement, Walt Rostow, believed that, with the reorganization of institutions and the undermining of traditional relationships, an economic "take-off" was possible—that is, a self-reinforcing system that, once set in motion, would continue to produce growth through the "miracle of compound interest" in an almost natural fashion. This theory was really selling a mirage. Nonetheless, there were numerous approaches to the economic take-off model, many of them equally dogmatic.

Some countries, following socialist models, pursued central planning. Others with or without planning opted to build steel mills and other heavy industries that, guarded by protective tariffs, they could grow in order to produce wealth and lead the country's entry into the developed world. Import substitution, the use of locally produced goods in the place of imported ones, became a byword for some of those proponents. Some, like leaders of the World Bank, argued for and supported infrastructural development, such as big dams and thermal power plants, to produce electricity, highways, harbors, and railroads. Others argued for investments in "human capital," which meant primarily investments in education. Some argued for balanced growth strategies. Others promoted development of leading sectors (Kuznets 1959; Hirshman 1958).

Some theorists insisted that, as long as less-developed countries were tied to the developed ones, they would always be at a disadvantage because of unequal terms of trade and the ways in which local elites exploited foreign investments for their own personal gains, defined narrowly (Frank 1979). This group of critics came to be called "dependency" theorists.

More recently, the World Bank, having discovered that big projects often failed, has been arguing for greater financial stringency on the part of governments, austerity programs, tight money, and limited activity, while also opening themselves up to freer trade.

Getting closer to the story of Southern's efforts in Arkansas, some nations have tried to use credit as a tool to encourage business growth. The government of India, for example, pushed its nationalized banks to make credit available to smaller businesses when it was against the inclinations of bankers to do so (Taub 1984).

During this same period, there was also a burgeoning community development movement. Community development was not necessarily economic development, but it might lead to it. Community developers tried to get community residents to work together to solve their problems, in some cases by actually contributing labor and, in others, working with government agencies to provide resources to help deal with locally identified problems. In some ways, community developers were doing what, in more recent times, has been called building social capital (Coleman 1988), developing the capacity of people to work together to achieve collective ends. Some of the people in this group were also particularly interested in improving the lot of exploited minorities and women.

Despite their ambiguous success in the third world, many of these strategies have been carried over into development for regions or states in the United Sates. The attraction of branch plants for big manufacturers, such as Mercedes-Benz and Honda, is similar to building heavy industry in the third world. In Arkansas, the rise of Nucor Steel is an example of this practice. All of the communities we looked at in Arkansas were trying to attract the branches of major companies, and in some cases they succeeded, although not always with wonderful results. Sanyo opened a plant in Forrest City, Arkansas, for example, but closed it again after repeated labor problems.

Arkadelphia attracted Carrier Air Conditioning; Petit Jean, a poultry processing plant and an airplane parts manufacturer that collected its incentives and then halted construction of its factory halfway through the building process as their business declined. The air-conditioning company did not do very well and never lived up to its expectation. Earlier, a ball-bearings plant, which located in the industrial park, closed up and moved on after its incentives were used up. Pine Bluff attracted a Japanese cable manufacturer.

It is the consensus among economists that communities that attract branches seldom earn back the level of subsidy they provided to get them there. And it is also true that often getting a company to build a branch in one place instead of another seems a little like robbing Peter to pay Paul. Nonetheless, they are popular with politicians because they provide lots of jobs. Jobs are the key. Forrest City even lobbied for and was awarded a state prison precisely for that purpose.

But jobs for local people may not be a consequence of the effort to attract branches in local communities. Most American-born people find working in poultry plants too distasteful for the low wages they provide. Temperatures are low. The floors are often wet. Viscera fly. And there is the danger of repetitive motion injury. As was the case in much of the south and southwest, poultry processing plants were quickly followed by the arrival of large numbers of Latin Americans who were willing to do the work. But their arrival often taxed the school systems that had historically been relatively homogeneous, yet now had to struggle with teaching English as a second language and the like.

Import substitution, which was also a strategy of Southern's, has been another tool developers have tried. States cannot follow this strategy by raising tariffs, as third world countries have often attempted to do. In this case, import substitution has involved the construction of networks of suppliers and customers so that companies or government agencies can purchase goods already produced in the state, instead of going outside for them. Or it may involve trying to encourage the production of a good that is heavily consumed locally but manufactured outside the region, causing an outflow of funds and jobs.

There is a great deal of effort to upgrade infrastructure, particularly as it pertains to means of transportation. Helena, which is situated on the Mississippi River, had built a port, and Pine Bluff had tried to develop its harbor area, as well. Helena and its neighboring cities lobbied to get an interstate highway built running north and south along the Mississippi. Arkadelphia had the road to town from a nearby interstate resurfaced when one company required it in order to locate there. With the rise of telecommunications and the Internet, there has also been an effort to improve communications.

Investments in education have long been a problem in the South, where local leaders thought that having an educated populace would raise the cost of labor (Wright 1986). There was a time not long ago when there were more great universities in the state of Illinois than there were in the whole South. Investments in higher education in poor states like Arkansas actually make it possible for more highly educated residents to leave the state in search of better opportunities. In Pine Bluff, it used to be said that graduates of the University of Arkansas campus there would come to graduation with a suitcase and a bus ticket to the North. Some southern states, such as North Carolina, however, have been able to use education as a development strategy. The most famous of these is the Research Triangle, where the University of North Carolina and Duke University have provided an anchor for a development area, focusing on scientific research.

As in the dependency theory discussed above, some have argued that places like Arkansas continue to be poor because local elites benefit, as they always have, from keeping the population down while they make money dealing with the large urban areas, mainly in the North. Historically such places, Arkansas included, have had a weak union movement as part of the low-wage strategy. Members of the Arkadelphia elite often explained to me that the reason Reynolds Aluminum closed was that they were unionized and labor costs became too high. Nowadays, though, workers were more realistic in their demands. At least one manufacturing employer in Arkadelphia was hostile to the Clark County Industrial Council because, with every branch plant it attracted, the wages of his workers had to go up.

Control of credit is another way to keep working-class populations down, making it difficult for them to start or grow their own businesses. Depriving them of credit may not be intentional. But the way in which banks make loans might have that consequence. For example, lending that emphasizes the character of the borrower or the borrower's family, rather than the nature of their business, excludes the people who are not known to the bankers from getting loans. This was believed to be the case in Arkansas and other southern towns where loan volume seemed relatively small. Visitors reported attending loan committee meetings where people said about loan applicants, "I know those folks. They are hard workers. And the Mrs. is not one of those extravagant people who wear fancy clothes and jewelry." One banker friend, whom I was trying to persuade to provide credit to a person whose formal criteria for credit was deficient, remarked in support of her loan, "I know that family. They would never miss a payment. Even if they had no money, they would go hungry before failing to pay off a loan."

The theory, then, is that, by extending credit to previously excluded groups, their situation will improve, and they will provide job opportunities for others. When one looks at the literature, it is not always clear what the outcome of extending credit is supposed to be. One goal is poverty alleviation, in which the beneficiaries are mainly those people who get the loans with some incidental gains of part-time jobs for those nearby. Another goal is to provide an economic motor that, in the spirit of Rostow's (1990) take-off, will have positive consequences for the whole economy of the region under consideration. It does seem to be the case that micro-loans—the very small ones made to the poorest people—do not provide jobs for people other than the loan recipients. To the extent that lives are better, it is because the loan made some economic improvement for one individual. There is very little evidence that these loans have multiplier effects through the larger community.

Although there is an enormous body of literature about micro-enterprise and its consequences, there is much less about using credit for larger businesses—that is, businesses with growth potential rather than those seen as mere opportunities for self-employment. There is even less about what stages of business are the most effective for producing economic growth. For example, it would be useful to know if loans are most successful at the stage where companies could ratchet themselves up to the next level because the loans would provide the kind of credit they need for a stepped-up level of growth through substantially enlarged customer orders or for bids on large contracts. And it would also be useful to compare this to support for start-ups, even though, outside of the high-tech corridors, there is no evidence to date suggesting that promising start-ups have the capacity to grow enough that they can either hire substantial numbers of local people or, themselves, provide new business opportunities for other local firms.

No one at Southern had this information. Nonetheless, the premise on which the organization was built was that credit would be the major tool to achieve development. There was also some conversation about the most appropriate types of business to give credit to, with a clear preference for manufacturing.

Possible Legal Constraints on Development Activities in the Southern Model

As discussed in chapter 2, the Southern Development Bancorporation and the Arkansas Enterprise Group (AEG) were, legally speaking, separate companies. They were created that way because not-for-profit and for-profit companies cannot legally be combined. If they were, one could see how the costs could be shifted to the for-profit, with the not-for-profit then avoiding taxes by taking the profits. On the other hand, a not-for-profit is legally eligible to receive grants from private foundations and government agencies. If funds designated for not-for-profit use were to enhance the profits of the for-profit unit, that would violate the intent of the law, which encouraged not-for-profit organizations and foundations to use those funds for otherwise unprofitable, but socially desirable, enterprises.

Consequently, two separate companies were created—one (Southern) having at its core a for-profit bank and for-profit real estate development corporation, and the other (AEG) having companies not expected to make money, but to do socially useful activities broadly defined. As discussed earlier, the core of AEG was a company designed to encourage entrepreneurship by providing seed capital for uncertain start-ups and by taking on riskier loans than a bank would dare to do—with the probability of a higher default rate than a bank, but also with the goal of producing some successful businesses that would become engines of development. This company would also perform other activities that might be expensive and would not provide an adequate rate of return—providing technical assistance, for example, such as helping people market their products. Another non-remunerative activity might be helping to change the climate about entrepreneurship in the region. In addition, the not-for-profit included the Good Faith Fund, for which the grants economy was essential (although, as I shall discuss, there was always the hope that the Good Faith Fund could be self-sustaining). The key point, however, is that Southern and AEG were created to work together in ways that would generate synergies in producing development outcomes. From the perspective of Chicago's management, both companies were created at the same time, with the same general management, in order to produce some kind of shared consequence.

However, there were two sets of issues concerning both organizations. On the one hand, there were the legal dimensions about the legitimate relations between the two companies. On the other, given the fact that these were, de jure, two companies, even with their separate boards, the local managers of each could assert independence from the other and argue for separate goals and interests. For example, if I, as an interviewer, happened to lump the two companies together as Southern, the AEG manger always corrected me. He perceived that he had more freedom of action vis-à-vis the for-profit, than did either the Chicago management or the community whose members saw them as the same company.

SECTION 23A

Relationships between banks and their affiliates are severely regulated matters. Under Section 23A of the Federal Reserve Act, for example, a bank may not purchase a low-quality asset from an affiliate. To the extent that a bank makes a loan to an affiliate, it must have at least 100 percent collateral. The quality of the loan must be assessed separately by the bank, and the bank must also be in the first position to collect on the loan. This was always taken very seriously by bank examiners, and regulations were tightened after the bank scandals of the late 1980s. For example, at one time one of the South Shore Bank's affiliates in Chicago was overdrawn on an account, and the bank paid out the check. This meant, in effect, that the bank had given its affiliate an uncollateralized loan. The company was taken to task on this by federal officials. To avoid such possibilities in the future, the bank required that its affiliates open accounts in unrelated banks. To the extent that the bank is involved in credit activities with an affiliate, there must be evidence that the bank had decided to make the loan on terms it determined independently of the affiliate.

In addition, there was supposed to be, according to legal advice, a wall between the two companies—particularly as regards economic matters. For example, both companies hoped that the business-development arm of AEG would generate growing businesses and that these would eventually out-grow the subsidized world and become regular bank customers. However, according to law, the not-for-profit could not force successful new businesses to turn to the Elk Horn Bank for finance. Because of all these constraints, extreme care was required when both organizations made loans to the same company.

LENDER LIABILITY

Although not legally connected to the for-profit/not-for-profit issues, the legal problem of lender liability interposes another constraint on the development process. As I have now repeatedly suggested, part of the process of doing development is both helping business people to be better at what they do if they are already in business and giving them guidance in getting businesses started. It seems clear that technical assistance is an important part of the process. That activity might only be showing an inexperienced company how to get its books in order—both as a way to get loans and to make business decisions. In the latter case, this includes the kinds of information needed to justify the purchase of a new piece of equipment, to expand or to take on a new technology, or to allocate resources differently among production and marketing. In the course of thinking over the trajectory for a business, one might suggest a consultant or even a new software package.

One potential problem is that, if the borrower's business fails, he or she can blame it on the lender: "The lender told me that I had to follow what turned out to be an unwise course in order to get the loan; and it was that course that forced me to fail." Under those circumstances—considered to be "inordinate control" by the law—the borrower may sue not only to be absolved from paying back the loan, but also to recover "damages." (Norton n.d.) One can see that this might pose a very large downside.

Among the behaviors that might be considered inordinate control are "direct interference with the day-to-day operations of the debtor; replacement of the debtor's management by management favorable to the lender; and coupling traditional lending objectives with other business goals" (Norton n.d., concerning Matthew Bender Co., 1–4, section 1.02–1.2003).

In some ways, as a development lender, one is potentially subject to all these charges. Elk Horn Bank and AEG lenders worked with businesses on their books, sent in experts to look over business processes and make recommendations, and even took on a kind of managerial responsibility. In at least three cases, AEG employees actually worked as quasi-employees/ consultants and in a quasi-managerial role. Bankers and borrowers argued about whether or not the borrowers needed or should have a particular piece of equipment, the appropriate size of a payroll, and whether or not they should expand into new space. In some instances, they encouraged some businesses to work with others. One should note that these prohibitions seldom apply in the case of venture capital investments based on the Southern Ventures model. Investors, as owners, have different rights. Indeed, in the agreements between Southern Ventures and its clients, conditions included the right to fire managers and hire others selected by the investors. In at least one case, Southern Ventures actually did this.

Traditional bankers may fear the possibility of lender liability lawsuits, because they want to eschew all risks. Indeed, this may be why traditional bankers cannot do development. They also may use this as an excuse not to do development. According to the legal experts I consulted who have tried both sides of those cases, lender liability cases are not very common, and they are particularly difficult to win. They require evidence of totally unreasonable pressure by the lender, or clear violation of previous agreements. One example of a successful lender liability lawsuit involved a bank that canceled a promised line of credit, even though the borrower was current with payments and complied with all requirements. The borrower argued that it was midway through a planned expansion program, and cutting off the flow of committed funds had dire business consequences. It is also the case, as well, that borrowers are accustomed to blaming lenders for their failures, the most common complaint being that the loan was too small. It takes a great deal more than that to win a lender liability lawsuit. Despite Southern's great participation in its customers' activities, only one such suit was brought against any of the organization's companies—in this case, Southern Ventures—and that one was settled. According to people involved in the case, the African American borrower, who operated a candy manufacturing company, only filed the suit in self-defense. He probably would not have brought the suit if Southern had not so aggressively tried to recoup its investment. The point of all this is that, in the relationships among the customers and on issues of potential lender liability, the company was willing to take the risks that were perceived to be essential in the development process—risks that perhaps set them apart from traditional bankers.

Normal banking procedure eschews such activity. Bankers as a group are risk averse, which means that, normally, in their efforts to avoid problems, they are unable to take the appropriate actions required to do real development activities. That risk-averse pattern militated against development activities in other ways. I have already discussed the fact that many bankers in Arkansas did not want to do SBA lending. In their eyes, either a loan was a good loan or it was not. That SBA lending made possible the opportunity to move slightly further out on a risk/reward curve and that it might also have provided funding opportunities for those otherwise excluded was not part of their thinking. Similarly, although there was a Small Business Administration program for working capital loans—that is, primarily money for raw materials or staff salaries—many local bankers were opposed to making them. On the one hand, they believed the working capital should come from normal cash flow. On the other, it made them nervous, because the collateral in such situations was unstable. For example, as the business used up the raw materials, they were no longer available for collateral; they could not be sold to recover the lent money. There can be steps taken to prevent that from happening. When banks lend money to car dealers, for example, in order to pay for the cars they get from the manufacturer, they make the loans for each individual car. As that car is sold, that part of the loan is paid off. In some cases, valuable raw materials are kept locked up, and as they are released for use or sale, the equivalent value of the loan is paid.

Yet, often it is just such a loan that enables a business to ratchet itself up to a new level. This is particularly true when one has both to demonstrate the capacity to deliver on a new, large order and, actually, to use the capacity—that is, the ability to purchase raw materials to fulfill the contract. The most successful working-capital loan the Elk Horn Bank made under the SBA working capital (Green Line) program was to a small sawmill that specialized in the production of hardwood flooring. In anticipation of a serious wood shortage and the constraints involved in aging wood before it can be processed, it used its loan to augment dramatically its wood supplies. Entering into a larger market successfully, it attracted a national purveyor of hardwood flooring which purchased the company. Another successful working-capital loan was to the manufacturer I discussed in chapter 3, who learned by chance on the high school soccer field that the Elk Horn Bank had loans available to him. Receiving one of those loans made his company's survival possible.

Thus, successfully doing development lending does involve taking on some of the sacred cows of traditional banking practices, but, at times, it also involves trying to work within a framework of law so structured that promising activities tend to get choked off. In Chicago, the Shorebank Corporation succeeded where conventional banking wisdom had insisted that one could not make money lending—particularly in real estate and in an African American community. At some points, even bank examiners had to be persuaded that lending money to African Americans with fledgling businesses was actually a good bet. Where people have been historically excluded for non-financial reasons (although sometimes clothed with a financial rationale)—that is, because of their race or some background factor—it is clear that making credit available to otherwise qualified borrowers is to provide that group with new economic opportunity. But this also means being involved with borrowers who are learning as they go or who are trying to move from limited, often personalistic, markets to more distant and unfamiliar terrain. It means trying to combine resources from different sources in a coordinated way, which involves moving beyond traditional patterns of behavior. And with that comes a certain element of risk. At one point during discussions of these issues, an AMS official concluded, finally, that he could not both lend money and provide technical assistance.

CHAPTER 5

The Search for Borrowers

If there had been a credit shortage in southern Arkansas, the assumption would be that a new credit supply operating under different auspices might produce a stampede from the credit starved. Yet, as we have seen, there was no such stampede.

Of course, some people did get the message, or, at least, a certain kind of message. This message was that some foolish Yankees had come down to Arkansas to give money away. A few people lined up to take their chances, but came up empty-handed because their deals were doubtful.

But, nonetheless, there was no queue for loans via the bank, via AEG, or via the Good Faith Fund. And, indeed, the history of the first eight years of the Southern Development Bank Corporation is the history of a search for doable deals. I will come back to the question about what one does under those circumstances. But the point is that, on its face, it would seem as if the initial diagnosis of a lack of credit availability is incorrect. One might make the case that a lack of enterprising banking over a long history might have contributed to Arkansas's economic plight—that the lack of available capital discouraged entrepreneurial initiative to such an extent that people stopped thinking of starting businesses as an option. One can think of the reluctance to make business loans over time as generating or supporting a non-entrepreneurial culture. However, there are many hypotheses for the lag in economic growth in the South in general, and the absence of aggressive credit provision is not, I believe, even on the list. On the other hand, there is a literature on conservative southern banking, so it may have some relevance after all. It is significant, perhaps, that part of the story of Arkansas's greatest entrepreneur, Sam Walton, involves his having the sense to marry the daughter of a banker, who provided him with credit when he opened his first store.

Members of both AEG and the Good Faith Fund did search for new customers. One Small Business Development Center official in Pine Bluff reported, "Those people [the employees of AEG] have shaken every tree and looked under every rock [for customers]. If they haven't found them, they are not there." Each company had people out there struggling to make loans. Trying to take their message to southeastern Arkansas, for example, AEG officials established "small business days," where all those agencies in the region with an interest in promoting small businesses would be available. Few candidates presented themselves. Loan officers visited local businesses to talk to businessmen who might know of something underway that would benefit from funding, and they mostly came up empty-handed. One person visited a temporary labor company, hoping that the owner's broad range of contacts would direct him to growing businesses needing credit.

Where loan opportunities could be found, many of the businesses were fragile. At one point, AEG officials were working very closely with three manufacturers, none of whom was ultimately able to succeed. One produced corrugated cardboard inserts for packaging. This type of product would seem theoretically ideal. One theory about promoting small companies is that it makes sense to find specialty or niche products in which the big economic powerhouses were not interested. This product certainly fit that specification. It also represented an alternative to that part of the environmental movement that was opposed to the use of expanded polystyrene in packaging. Yet, despite being propped up with funding over a six-year period and being supplied with advice about cost cutting, pricing, and management, the company was unable to survive. The same was true for a company trying to sell household and gift products, such as lamp bases, crafted out of wood. A third manufactured doors and aimed its product nationally at public housing and apartment buildings. In each case, in addition to providing funding, AEG employees worked very closely with the manufacturers over a long period of time but were not able to turn these companies around.

An employee of Southern Ventures spent six months working with a minority entrepreneur whose business consisted of testing for radioactive waste from facilities that processed nuclear products. This businessman was buttressed by laws requiring bidders on large contracts to engage some proportion of minority subcontractors. Yet, even with the company in a somewhat protected position, she was unable to save it.

Minority lending and investing was a special problem. That goal had been an important focus at the time of Southern's creation. In fact, the original effort to locate in the Delta, which has a majority African American population, had been shaped by that commitment. Indeed, in the early years, some whites stayed away from the organization because they thought it was a bank for blacks only. However, within the framework of committing itself to south Arkansas, Southern was unable to find many minority borrowers. At that time, Southern Ventures had a minority employee who proposed that she make minority investing her special responsibility. Her subsequent analysis demonstrated that there were so few minority businesses in southern Arkansas that, for her to be effective, she would have to enlarge the target area to include Little Rock (Pulaski County) and Lonoke County, to the north and east. Even with that extension of territory, she was not able to generate much volume.

The Elk Horn Bank also hired a minority lender whose primary task was to find African American business people to whom to lend money. She also traversed a large area trying to find customers, but with modest success and mixed results.

Most of the loans made to African Americans were made by African Americans. Between 1988 and 1996, Elk Horn Bank originated fifty-seven development loans to minority businesses for a total of $4.7 million. For most of the eight years in which this study was being conducted, with the exception of the Good Faith Fund, there were only between two and four African American employees in the Elk Horn Bank, Southern Ventures, and AEG combined who were qualified to make those loans. Because of the difficult economic situation for African Americans in Arkansas, these lenders often reported feelings of frustration in trying to generate business.

The Good Faith Fund manager, whose difficulty in finding customers I will discuss in detail below, at one point proposed extending the target area to Little Rock as a strategy to increase loan volume. Her idea was also that Little Rock had a more vibrant economy than the areas in southern Arkansas and that this expansion of region would have the potential of producing more black candidates for self-employment.

In order to generate volume, then, all of the companies moved outside their original market areas. There were loans as far away as Mena, on the western edge of the state, and Blytheville, in the northeastern part of the state. Of course, the Elk Horn Bank was still functioning as a local bank, and, with most of the resources, it made most of the loans. And most of those could not be considered development lending. By development lending I mean loans to people who could not get them elsewhere to start a new business, or to people moving their business up to a new level. It excludes single-family house mortgages, consumer loans, and loans to already successful small businesses.

Southern Ventures also did one of its deals outside the southern part of the state as far away as Northwest Arkansas. AMS and the Good Faith Fund had been creative in finding new sources of lending dollars. But it was not easy to lend them effectively to achieve development. The lack of concentrated activity works against real economic growth for a region.

Creating Loan Products and Related Issues

Southern's employees not only traveled widely trying to find good deals, but also were inventive in creating loan products as well. In a particularly creative move, AMS invented "working capital investments" to kill two birds with one stone. The two "birds" were the state of Arkansas's usury law and the difficulty of making working capital loans to small uncertain businesses.

The usury law set interest rates at five points above the federal discount rate, which, in practice, came to about two points over prime. A basic rule in lending money is that the rate of interest should be related to the amount of risk. By setting a ceiling on loan interest rates, Arkansas's usury law made this impossible, making somewhat risky loans uneconomic to make, thereby placing a constraint on organizations like AMS, which were in the business of financing companies somewhat further out on the risk curve than ordinary banks would normally undertake. In fact, Arkansas bankers made this argument against the usury law every time it came up for reconsideration. They agreed that bankers did not invest adequately in Arkansas businesses. But they argued that, with the usury law constraint, they could not do so profitably. If they could charge more interest, they could invest more freely in businesses, and that would improve the Arkansas economy.

The Southern companies were up against the same problem. The second bird here was how to make working capital loans to very small businesses. One way of dealing with that problem is to lock up raw materials and only release a certain amount per day or per week as the loan gets paid down. That was precisely the practice of banks in India, even those with programs to encourage small businesses. (Taub 1989). It is a common practice in England, as well, and not unheard of in this country. But it is a program difficult to implement with small quantities of materials of not very great value.

The challenge, then, was to find a way to make working capital loans to small companies in ways in which interest rates would compensate for risk. These small companies are the ones who find working capital difficult to come by and are therefore constrained from growing. Working capital investments were an ingenious solution to both problems.

This is the way they were structured. A customer would bring in a contract or purchase order to deliver a certain product within a specified time frame. AMS would help purchase the raw materials—that is, make an investment directly in the necessary raw materials. In return, AMS would then share in the profit after the product was sold, in the same way that an investor would, and quite differently from a banker, who would try to collect on the loan whether or not the goods were sold. The idea would be that, over the course of a year, several of these deals would occur as the manufacturer found new orders in which raw material funding was required. The investment for each discrete contract was defined as a separate joint venture. Under this plan, AEG did not hold a security interest in the purchased assets, nor would it charge an interest rate. The average starting investment was planned to be around $2,000, with the expectation that future investments might increase to $25,000.

Because each deal was an investment rather than a loan, AEG was able to earn a higher rate of return than it would have if it were making a loan. In this case, the goal was to produce a yield of about five points above prime. In the first six months of the program, the company made several such investments. One, an investment of $1,548, went to a company that provided souvenirs—inscribed pens, notebooks, and caps for events such as conventions and family reunions. Another, an investment of $5,384, went to a sausage manufacturer for the purchase of animals to be subsequently slaughtered. And the third, $11,387, went to a manufacturer of file folders. In addition, $17,000 went to a company that made kitchen equipment for fast food manufacturers. This company went bankrupt during the first year of the program.

As one can see, there were people who were willing to buy into the program because they were so credit constrained. But there were problems with this. Earlier I discussed the fact that a company arriving in town with a new program has to send out a clear message. As innovative as this program was, it was also poorly understood and sometimes sent the wrong message. Venture partners let it be known that they were paying what, in their minds, were interest rates in excess of 15 percent, fueling the belief held by many that the do-good message being sent by the company was a cover for exploitation. And at least one such partner, professing not to understand the distinctive properties of the investment process, took the money allotted to raw material and purchase and used it for capital improvements. In his case, instead of buying hogs, he purchased refrigerators and display cases. The resulting controversy over the matter left a bad taste both for the participants and other people who knew or came to know the story. The partner in question was quite certain that he had not done anything wrong, and reported that he was offended by one of the AMS principals whom, he claimed, called him a crook. On the other hand, having nothing to sell because he did not use the money to buy raw material to convert into sausage, he had no direct profits to pay back the investment. He finally did work out a long-term pay-back schedule.

Another partner-client was so irked by the process that, although she followed the correct procedures, she felt exploited. Later, she found herself in a position where her negative sentiments about the company may have had consequences.

Part of the problem here relates back to the complex ideas concerning the entering message of Southern. On several occasions, I interviewed samples of borrowers or customers of the Southern companies. One continuing and surprising finding was that satisfaction with the company's business dealings was inversely related to knowledge about its special mission. Those who received loans through more or less normal business routes felt that, compared to other lenders they had dealt with, Southern was just fine. They were even grateful that they were able to get financing from those offices when others had turned them down. Those who came to Southern companies because they had heard about its special mission to encourage economic growth by encouraging small businesses often felt exploited and rubbed the wrong way.

AMS had other problems. Despite its early mandate to create conditions that would facilitate the development of small business through technical assistance, it was never able to deliver attractive and usable programs. Instead, it became primarily a lending organization, struggling to earn as much of its operating budget as it could. It did make attempts to provide technical assistance; but—feeling constrained by its economic position—it wanted and needed to sell that technical assistance. For example, a person was hired to produce a handbook or guide to marketing. The theory was that this document would be sold to those needing assistance. There were few customers. Providing technical assistance to small-scale entrepreneurs is a special problem. One must remember that many people who choose to start their own businesses are independent types—that is one of the reasons they are entrepreneurs instead of employees. They often believe that they know their business better than anybody else, and they are loathe to take guidance from outsiders—especially outsiders who do not have a track record in "their" businesses. In research on entrepreneurs that I conducted in India, small-scale manufacturers often asked me that, if technical assistance providers were so good, why had they not become rich in their own businesses?

Small businessmen struggling with day-to-day problems also believe that their businesses have special features that nobody else could truly understand—or that solutions tried elsewhere would not work for them. There is a useful distinction to be made between generic advice and business-specific advice. To an outsider, a good bookkeeping program could apply to a great range of situations. The small businessman is not a generalist, and he needs solutions to his problems as he sees them. He is also suspicious of people who do not run their own businesses. What could they possibly know? Everybody knows that the things you learn from books are not useful in the real world. Following from this is the fact that most small entrepreneurs are not bookish types. Reading long and detailed instructions is just not their style. The likelihood that they would pay for advice from an outsider, especially advice presented in a detailed book format, was very small. And, indeed, this proved to be the case.

AMS also tried to sell an accounting software package. It, too, met with market resistance, although some borrowers were persuaded to make use of the package. It is important to understand that many of these small businesses did need the assistance promised by these packages. After careful review of their businesses, for example, it was discovered that at least two borrowers from the whole Southern operation sold items for less than the cost to produce or purchase them. And it was also true that many small businesses had little understanding of marketing beyond the world they knew in Arkansas; under the proper circumstances, advice about how to improve marketing to that world could have been useful to them. Nonetheless, AMS felt that the main way it could deliver such help in an economically sensible fashion was to make it generic—applicable to an array of business types—and then sell it.

AMS management tried other tools as well. The most interesting, perhaps, was a program to provide a central Visa charge facility for small businesses that attempted to market their products outside the immediate area. The first manufacturer who participated in this program was the producer of just the kind of product that should have been a success. A local automobile upholsterer designed an all-weather compartment for hunters and farmers who made use of four-wheelers, which, like motorcycles, leave the driver in an exposed position. Mounted on a fiberglass frame connected to the vehicle, the compartment was constructed of wind-resistant and waterproof fabric with a plastic window (much like the rear window in a convertible car) through which the driver could see. This seemed like an ideal case for encouraging local entrepreneurship as the manufacturer produced a product for local conditions but that product would also have an appeal beyond the small immediate market.

The manufacturers had a clear understanding of their two major types of consumers: farmers who make use of four-wheelers to traverse their lands and hunters who make use of those vehicles to gain access to difficult terrain. There were numerous farms in the region, and southwest Arkansas is the sort of place where the schools close when hunting season opens. These manufacturers, then, were producing a good for a market they knew and understood. They had won a placement in a large national catalog that specialized in products for hunters. But their sales volume was not high enough for them to continue in that advantageous position after the first year. AMS helped with research on the kinds of magazines hunters and farmers read, and they helped place advertisements in those journals. It is not clear that there were sufficient orders to keep this enterprise going or that the manufacturers, who operated a few sewing machines in a garage, could keep up with orders and maintain quality. The local evaluation of the product was that it looked flimsy. But, whatever the reason, both the credit card project and the four-wheeler projects fizzled.

In the initial conception of AEG, there had been hope that the discovery of exciting ways to encourage business growth, outside of simply making loans, might intrigue foundations and help produce other possible sources of funds. To that end, one of AEG's first employees was a development specialist whose job was to act as a liaison with foundations and similar personnel and to help in the process of raising operating funds. Obviously, Shorebank management in Chicago had great success raising money from eleemosynary institutions. They funded a large part of the costs of doing business in Chicago and were totally responsible for the capitalization of Southern. In creating the organizational structure in Arkansas, the role of development officer had been included because the Shorebank managers believed it would be a normal part of the process. Although the AMS management was skilled at finding government programs that provided loan funds, it never connected to the conception the Chicago management team brought with them. The development officer did raise some money. But, after about two years with the company, she was let go, and the position was never refilled.

After a series of failures of this type, AMS left the technical assistance business in a direct and formal sense. It must be noted, however, that its employees over the years devoted a great deal of time, energy, and resources to assist their clients, with some of them spending weeks in customers' shops taking measurements, making observations, and working on the books.

One possible way to provide technical assistance to small manufacturers is to create conditions under which they choose their consultants and, ultimately, to help pay for them. This procedure overcomes some of the difficulties with generic advice and uncertainty about advice quality that small businesses face. AMS participated in one other, more indirect, effort at technical assistance that helped to surmount these problems. Having seen that a local metalworkers' network appeared to be successful, AMS teamed up with the developer of that network and a local, but internationally renowned, economic development organization to produce a business network for wood-products producers. The calculations behind it made sense. If small businesses would not take advice from outsiders of doubtful provenance, perhaps they would from each other—particularly if they were led by somebody who had experience in the wood-products business. And those were the conditions the network set out to create. A woodworkers' network was established with resources from the international development organization and an economic contribution from AMS, with guidance from the man who had created the metalworkers' network. A local individual who had wood-products experience was chosen to lead it. Unfortunately, all of the main actors had different conceptions of how the organization should operate and where primary responsibility for its operation should lie. There were also tensions over who deserved the credit for the organization's creation. It, too, never achieved its promise.

In summary, one can see that AMS management was inventive and energetic in trying to provide both technical assistance and new ways to make loans. Management believed that it did not have enough money to go into technical assistance in a big-time, non-revenue-producing way (instead, perhaps, of devising exciting schemes and going to the foundation world for support), and most of its efforts at innovation were not productive.

Ultimately, then, AMS became a lending organization. Under pressure to support itself, it cast about for loan opportunities and, in so doing, distributed its efforts far beyond any reasonable conception of a targeted area. Some of the loans were made in tandem with the other companies. For example, a company that had developed a process for coating steel to protect it from high friction operations, such as spinning yarn, which had initially been a Southern Ventures investment, was subsequently a loan customer of AMS, as well. Indeed, that loan and investment was one of the successes for both subsidiaries.

There were other loans that were successful, as well. For example, a company that smoothed, polished, and shaped Arkansas sharpening stones borrowed money to help produce new packages to improve marketing. Starting out in a garage with a few old grinding tools, it was able, subsequently, to move into new quarters, increasing its business and doubling the number of its employees.

A banking cliché is that all loans look good when they are made. But it is also true that bad loans may take some time to make their failures apparent. In the search for companies that might grow and have an impact on the surrounding area, AMS made important loans to what seemed to be promising companies, only to see several of them fail. The list of companies that failed is large.

These include some of the companies I have already described: the company that made corrugated inserts to stabilize items and protect items being shipped in cases and the company that made decorative items out of wood. Others on the list included a company that made wire harnesses for electronic equipment and a company that manufactured doors, with the hope that sales could be made both to big, home-building supply companies and public housing authorities (this one received extensive assistance, but, nonetheless, over a long period of time, gradually died). Yet another company put together upscale puzzle packages and sold art posters from European museums. This company was the authorized U.S. representative for those items for the Prado Museum in Madrid. When I first visited this business, there was no machinery. Puzzles arrived partially cut, and employees broke them apart and put them in boxes. Over time, the company increased its capacity to make its own puzzles, purchasing items such as die-cutting machines. However, they may have expanded too aggressively and they, too, after more than five years of support, failed. Again, one sees that AMS, in the process of searching for viable customers, selected interesting companies to lend money to and stayed with them for some time in the hope that operations would improve. Yet, in too many cases, the companies failed.

Southern Ventures

Southern Ventures was characterized by tough, enterprising management. Its manager wanted to put muscle behind the development process by finding exciting companies with rapid growth prospects and helping to guide them to great economic success. The venture capital world is where one often finds the cowboys and macho men. Normally, bankers want little to do with the management of their customers' companies, and they are constrained from doing much by law anyway. Following a common practice among investors in venture capital companies, Southern Ventures management put itself on the boards of its clients and wrote contracts in which it gave itself the power to remove managers if they did not perform adequately. This was not the only possible approach to this kind of activity. Indeed, one Shorebank board and Southern board member, who himself was a successful venture capitalist, did not think this was a good policy. He felt that this approach created enemies out of people who should be partners, and that it also encouraged less than full disclosure of information by clients, particularly if the news was bad, thus making it difficult to work on new strategies should the company get into trouble. He defined his own role when doing venture capital as being more of a cheerleader.

When the Southern Ventures manager realized how much managerial assistance the client companies required, he hired a consultant who had been a successful entrepreneur in the knitting and hobby-craft industry to work with specific companies.

Nonetheless, Southern Ventures entered into the process with great gusto, in many cases finding interesting companies—often surprising technologically for rural south Arkansas. Among the most successful was the investment described in the report on AMS in chapter 2, the manufacturer who produced coatings to reduce friction on high-speed, moving parts of manufacturing equipment. Also included in this group was a company called Hot Metal Molding that produced cast aluminum parts, primarily for the automobile industry, utilizing a technology that included squeezing the molten material into molds.

Losses included a technologically advanced waste-water treatment facility; an advanced petroleum refining company; and a company that did radioactive assays for companies that made use of radioactive materials. Others included a company that produced kitty litter and one that manufactured cooking and storage equipment for fast food establishments. On the scale of venture capital activity, this record of hits and misses was not unusual. Venture capitalists often expect the majority of their investments to fail, with the profits from the successes more than making up for those losses. But venture capitalists also usually work with deeper pockets. Capitalized at $1.25 million, Southern Ventures did not leave much margin for error. Efforts to augment that amount with the help of outside partners largely failed. The company was never able to achieve meaningful participation with the Small Business Administration, which preferred strategies that made use of credit rather than investment. And other possible partners, such as the Arkansas Development Finance Authority, declined to participate. What made matters worse was that the Southern Ventures manager used some of the scant resources he had available for investing in a single effort to keep one of the companies afloat. Like other companies, Southern Ventures was forced to pursue deals beyond the targeted area in order to gain volume. About half of Southern Ventures' deals were in Little Rock or its suburbs, and one (which did have real rural development consequences) was a far north as Springdale. If one were to use venture capital as a tool of rural development in the future, the challenge would be to find some way to use the venture capital mechanism only within a targeted or focused area when the rare appropriate occasion arises, without having to support a whole company whose sole reason for existence is to find appropriate venture deals—for in that way lies distortion.

In 1993, the company was unofficially bankrupt, with losses of $951,000 and a negative net worth of $522,900. Some of those losses, but not all, were subsequently retrieved.

This manager never lost his sense of being a cowboy. After a brilliant report on a particular company failure, he reported on his relations to other companies by declaring, "We will just ride them hard and tight." But, with the discovery of the final magnitude of the losses, he resigned to become a partner and CEO of Hot Metal Molding, the aluminum casting company mentioned previously, which went on to do well and was eventually sold at a handsome profit for Southern Ventures. The company also went on to realize significant gains from two other investments.

The Good Faith Fund

The Good Faith Fund was the most imaginative and courageous element of the entire Southern program. Conceived of as an effort to make very small loans to very poor people and modeled after a program in Bangladesh, the fund followed a route that was relatively untested in the United States. Although it was risky, it was also the program whose elements captured the attention and enthusiasm of outside commentators. The program had elements that played well in American society. The goal was to encourage entrepreneurship among low-income people, encouraging their economic independence, providing a path of upward mobility, and, consequently, encouraging individual pride.

As Tocqueville and other observers of the American scene have pointed out over the years, Americans admire entrepreneurs—"the self-made men"—particularly those who "pull themselves up by their own boot straps." Such a program also gathers supporters when it appears to be cheap. Instead of grants, people get loans that they pay back with interest. The loans themselves revolve—the same money gets used over and over again, and the interest payments, according to those who express the most devoted admiration for this program, help to cover the costs of operation. Peer groups of borrowers also come together in many of these programs and, among other things, provide a form of support and guidance. According to some observers, this replaces the need for technical assistance. Some observers imagine these programs to be perpetual-motion machines that, once set in motion, will fund themselves as they move people up from poverty. The word from Bangladesh, Indonesia, and Latin America was that this is just what the programs did. And because peer-group-oriented, micro-enterprise lending programs, which were popular in India and elsewhere in Asia, encourage both individual entrepreneurship and group cooperation, they have had broad appeal here in the United States. In this model, small groups of individuals determine who among them will get loans, put pressure on each other to pay those loans back, and provide fellow members with moral support and advice. Loan amounts tend to be small and are meant to provide the borrower with the means to begin or expand a business enterprise. Nobody else in the group can get a loan until the first one is almost fully paid back. Consequently, group pressure replaces collateral and legal sanctions in encouraging repayment.

The idea that one might be able to transfer such a program to the United States has distinctive appeal. Among some people, there is a special charm in the idea that a rich country could learn something valuable about making wealth from a poor one, and any program that promises to help poor people climb out of poverty, costs little, and encourages individual entrepreneurship has clear appeal to American values. The Grameen Bank in Bangladesh, the best known of these programs, has become almost a holy place, although there are other loan funds that predate it, and others that are larger. Grameen boasts hordes of customers (two million in 1994) and a very high payback rate (over 95 percent), in the context of the tremendous poverty of Bangladesh (Bornstein 1996). These factors, along with the obvious brilliance and charisma of Grameen's founder, Muhammad Yunus, make Dhaka a pilgrimage destination for many.

Clearly, there is something about these programs that cries out to the American spirit. Perhaps the idea of peer-group lending balances a tension between the values of individualism and the need for community, about which Bellah et al. (1985) and others have reported: on one hand, the borrower-participant is an intrepid entrepreneur building individual wealth independently; on the other, he or she gains strength and knowledge from the support and encouragement of a community-like group that makes it possible to move on and to succeed. Nevertheless, the amount of public enthusiasm these programs generate is significantly out of proportion to their actual ability to foster economic development and growth. The appeal of that imagery led to great public attention for the Good Faith Fund, modeled after the Grameen Bank, far more than any other aspect of the Southern program. The real story, alas, is one of very limited success. The Good Faith Fund improved the lives of only a small group of low- and moderate-income working families. This is a worthwhile achievement, but a far cry from getting large numbers of people off welfare or achieving economic development.

To understand what happened to the Good Faith Fund, one needs to know more about the Grameen Bank and its practices. I will provide a brief summary of the Grameen Bank to help build some minimal understanding of its program. Only by doing that can we better understand the difficulties that the Good Faith Fund faced.

THE GRAMEEN BANK

Group membership is central to the Grameen Bank program. Loans are made by the bank, through its area-level representatives, to individuals in groups. Because the members presumably do not have adequate collateral, group social pressures force them to pay the loan back. That is, a second person in the group cannot get a loan until the first loan is substantially repaid. In addition, groups often have collective savings accounts, and members may make some kind of deposit each time they meet. Members use the loans to operate some kind of business, called, in the language of the peer-group-lending trade, micro-enterprises. In Bangladesh, common loans might be for the purchase of a cow, making it possible to sell milk to neighbors, or a rice-husking machine, also for local commerce. Groups also provide moral support and encouragement, as well as advice.

Many of the Asian and South American programs, including Grameen's, try to limit their loans to the really poor. Grameen Bank requires its rural, poor, loan recipients to be landless and at the bottom of the economic pyramid. Micro-loan funds also appear to be disproportionately programs for women; the Grameen Bank has had mainly women customers (more than 90 percent) at this point, and most of the members of the American group have been female as well.

The Grameen operation is more than just a bank. It is a morally tinged activity with some of the flavor of a social movement. Groups meet approximately once a month; meetings boost morale and encourage the sharing of ideas. Meetings also serve to remind members of an array of moral tenets to which they committed themselves when they joined the group. These tenets are as follows:

1. The four principles of Grameen Bank: Discipline, Unity, Courage, and Hard Work. We shall follow and advance [these principles] in all walks of our lives.
2. Prosperity we shall bring to our families.
3. We shall not live in dilapidated houses . . .
4. We shall plant vegetables all year round. We shall eat plenty . . .
5. . . . [W]e shall plant as many seedlings as possible.
6. We shall plan to keep our families small.
7. We shall educate our children.
8. We shall build and use pit-latrines.
9. We shall drink tubewell water.
10. We shall not take any dowry in our sons' weddings, neither shall we give any dowry in our daughters' weddings . . .
11. We shall not inflict any injustice to anyone.
12. For higher income we shall collectively undertake bigger investments.
13. We shall always be ready to help each other.
14. If we come to know of any breach of discipline . . . we shall go there and help restore discipline.
15. We shall introduce physical exercise in all of our centers. (Bornstein 1996)

Obviously, these dicta represent a social program that extends far beyond what we would think of as economic transactions. The chanting of them before a meeting has a quasi-religious quality, and clearly the goals represent a broad social agenda in addition to immediate economic exchange. The point of this is that the Grameen Bank is not just a bank, and the micro-loans program provides not only the capital necessary to improve one's lot in life, but also the behaviors and attitudes that will mark one as no longer a member of the poorest segment of society. In the days of the British Empire, this was called social uplift.

TRIAL AND ERROR

Of that group, the Good Faith Fund became one of the best known. However, like many other peer-group-oriented, micro-enterprise loan funds in the United States, particularly those in rural areas, the Good Faith Fund was never able to deliver a meaningful volume of customers, to provide substantial loan services to the really poor, or to achieve anything close to institutional self-sufficiency. To the extent that it continues to survive and, perhaps, even to grow, it will do so by engaging in activities that do not appear to replicate the Grameen Bank example.

The story of the Good Faith Fund was one of trial and error, experiment and innovation, as its participants tried to figure out how to transplant the Grameen Bank approach to the southern United States. By the end of 1998, few of the original Good Faith Fund practices remained. In discussing the other components of Southern, we have already encountered many of the problems the Good Faith Fund faced. These included issues that were natural to new organizations anywhere, particularly those that lend out money: they were dealing with a historically oppressed population and they were being run by people not native to the area and thus unfamiliar with both local customs and the local people. These problems were compounded by the fact that many of the early employees of the Good Faith Fund were white and not from rural backgrounds. It takes time, experience, and contacts to identify serious and honest customers.

Just as with the other programs of Southern, the message that the Good Faith Fund had to deliver was complicated and did not fit into the target populations' understandings of how the world worked. Historically, white people, particularly in the South, have not been known to make financial deals in the interests of low-income African Americans. This is a classic "beware of Greeks bearing gifts" problem. In addition, in a world in which gifts and grants are what you do for the poor, a loan that must be paid back with interest seems a little strange. It is an odd creature, indeed, that announces that it will lend money at market rates—and characterizes this practice as a favor—even if credit at anything like those rates is not available elsewhere. (As previously noted, an Arkansas usury law set limits on rates of interest. Most successful micro-credit programs in Asia lend money at about twelve points over the going rate, which is considerably higher than Arkansas permits but is still substantially lower than what an Asian village money-lender would charge.) Many of the early prospective participants thought that the program meant that the fund would lend—or give—money to anyone with a good idea; they felt they had been misled when they had to produce business plans, complete financial prospectuses, and the like. This made communication very difficult and misunderstandings common.

The Good Faith Fund began its program with practices similar to those of the Grameen Bank. At the outset, the fund did not require collateral or credit checks, with the intention that, as with Grameen, group pressure would serve to encourage timely repayment of loans. Lending groups were supposed to meet approximately twice a month; there were also center meetings where multiple groups came together.

Among those who run peer-group lending programs for micro-enterprise, there is disagreement about whether or not to provide technical assistance. To the extent that self-sufficiency of the program is an organizational goal, the costs of providing technical assistance reduce the probability that the goal will be achieved. And there are arguments that suggest that technical assistance is unnecessary. For example, it is asserted that group members know best what is appropriate for their business conditions; that local business people are inventive and resourceful; and, therefore, that technical assistance is an unnecessary expense. The Good Faith Fund began without providing such assistance, but, over time, the program came to require that all micro-loan borrowers complete a six-week, small-business training program. In addition, centers sometimes invited guest speakers to talk about legal requirements of businesses or issues around income tax.

The volume of loans provided by the Good Faith Fund was small. In 1989 through 1992, the Good Faith Fund averaged eighteen new loan customers a year in its peer-group, micro-loan program. The following two years, the numbers peaked into the mid-twenties, dropping down dramatically after that, partly because of a change in management and a change in focus. In keeping with the Grameen Bank model, the average loan was small; for the first four years, it was just under $1,600. In 1989—one of the two years with a 48 percent default rate—the average loan was $3,176.

It became apparent that a certain unspecified amount of default in these years was due to apparent fraud by borrowers, and program management came to understand that, group process or no group process, credit checks should be made, collateral was essential if a loan (or whatever the loan purchased) was to be recovered, and that the fund ought to make payments directly to the purveyor of the goods purchased rather than to the borrower, in order to ensure that borrowed money was spent for its intended purpose. As another consequence of the high default rate, program managers decided to reduce the size of initial loans so that, given the cash flow and economic precariousness of borrowers, they would not have too much difficulty paying the loan back in the first year. These measures dramatically reduced loan losses and delinquencies. In 1993 and 1994, loan losses came down to 11 percent a year.

There were some success stories coming out of the Good Faith Fund's micro-loan program, even though most of the loans from this program went to providing services, rather than goods, which has its own complications to be discussed below. In my sample of respondents, there was an infant-care provider, an upholsterer, a beauty shop owner, a dressmaker and seamstress specializing in garments made in an African style, janitorial services and gardening services, and a caterer. The only respondents who actually sold a product sold Mary Kay cosmetics—a national company that specializes in a highly localized form of marketing.

One success is illustrated by the case of Thomasina Judge (the names of all borrowers are pseudonyms). Judge operated an infant day-care center, from what could most optimistically be called a sagging house with peeling paint. Watching Judge with her infant charges—feeding them, burping them, or just giving them a hug—was to watch somebody performing her metier. Judge had previously held a job that required her to work part time and in split shifts at minimum wage. She took home about $500 a month. Her husband was a laborer who also worked at a level close to minimum wage. Judge's experience with the Good Faith Fund was nothing but positive. The six-week training program was of great value to her. "I had this dream," she said, "and I did not know how to start. The Good Faith Fund showed me my first step, and then led me down the path."

Not only did the fund managers train her, but they answered her questions and then they lent her $900 (her first loan), followed by $1,200 to enable her to begin fixing up her house, install central heating and air conditioning, and purchase the cribs, playpens, and toys she needed to be in business. After a year, she was earning twice as much as she had in her previous job. Three years later she had doubled that. She had been able to put money into further fixing up her house and to fence her yard so that older children could play safely. However, not long after she received her first loan, she stopped going to group meetings. The meetings, she said, were "not much help to me." But the group had completely evaporated anyway.

Judge had only good things to say about the Good Faith Fund and the people who serviced her loan. "I feel they are still behind me, and still available. The way my life is now, I am not bogged down by bills. I have a better outlook for life. . . . I love children and I am doing what I always wanted to do." The Good Faith Fund enabled her to earn money doing something she liked, and it provided her with the means to supplement the household income to a greater degree than the job she had held previously. But it is not clear that her activities contributed to the economic development of the region.

The most successful graduate of the program was Beatrice Newsome, an African American who had worked in a dry cleaning plant in town and subsequently decided to open her own dry cleaning service—originally as a pick-up and drop-off service. A loan of $1,000 from the Good Faith Fund got her started. Ultimately, she borrowed $35,000 to purchase her own establishment, where she installed her own dry cleaning plant. In 2003, her business continued to do well. She was one of the few borrowers in the Good Faith Fund program who made the transition from micro-business to business. During our original interview, she made the point that the original loan was no big deal and that she could have gotten the resources elsewhere. Her husband was employed at a local government center. As with all of the successful borrowers I interviewed, a spouse or another member of the family produced a regular income via salary at the time that the Good Faith Fund loan was made.

Despite the changes the managers of the Good Faith Fund made, and despite the success stories that can be told, the problems that persisted suggest that wholesale transplantation of the Grameen Bank model to the United States—in particular, transplantation of the specific practices of that model—did not work. There are several reasons for this, each of which I will explicate in turn. They are (1) the meaning and practice of group activities; (2) population density and establishing a micro-loan program; (3) poverty conditions and the amount of capital, and the skills, necessary to alleviate those conditions; and (4) the safety net.

THE MEANING AND PRACTICE OF GROUP ACTIVITIES

During the early phases of the program, individuals were expected to bring already formed groups made of non-relatives to the Good Faith Fund. Given population densities, employment habits, and community expectations, very few people were able to produce four friends who also wanted to start businesses. Good Faith Fund personnel observed that individuals who arrived in the office requesting information about the program and were told to return with four friends simply did not do it. In response, the fund initiated a group-training program for all new members. Under revised rules, people could sign up for the training programs without being part of a preexisting group. After individuals completed the six-week training program, fund managers helped individuals construct groups. Needless to say, this kind of group, often constructed of strangers who had known each other only a few weeks, vitiated the supposed effects of group pressures. Belonging to such an artificially constructed group was not the same as belonging to one previously embedded in a community with strong preexisting social ties—one where social sanctions and other group pressures were likely to be effective.

Not only were Good Faith Fund group members relatively ineffective in putting pressure on each other, but they had trouble even holding together as groups over time. In our interviews with loan officers from the program, we asked them what their biggest problems were: groups falling apart was one consistent answer.

Respondents reported that, although meetings were pleasant and sometimes useful, there were so many other things to do in life that this was not a high priority. By that time, through another reformulation of the program, group members were not impeded in getting loans if other members failed to pay. This program alteration for the fund signified a realization that group pressure simply would not work as a motivation for getting people to repay loans. Some people explained they were reluctant to join a group if that meant either that they had some responsibility for someone else's behavior or that they would have to rely on somebody else to get what they needed. This step reduced the significance of group membership a great deal; the one shred of the original program left was that group members might be able to give each other moral support and a kind of commonsense technical assistance.

Toward the end of 1994, the Good Faith Fund began to take on a new and quite different look. Group lending played a small role, as its managers had come to see that a literal translation of the Grameen program did not work in southern Arkansas. Through successive iterations, efforts were made to make the fit better, and they are at a new place today. There continued to be a micro-enterprise loan fund, which the borrowers collectively played a large role in operating, but that fund began to play a smaller role in total operations than it did in the past. Instead, there were loans made to larger companies as a means of doing economic development and generating income for the fund.

POPULATION DENSITY, PRODUCTION, DISTRIBUTION, AND MARKETS

Why was it difficult to find potential customers, to say nothing of group members, for the Good Faith Fund? One answer is that, compared to Bangladesh, population densities in Arkansas are very low. The population in Bangladesh is 814 per kilometer. In the five counties served by the Good Faith Fund (Jefferson, Lincoln, Desha, Chicot, and Ashley), the population is 36.0, 9.0, 8.0, 9.1, and 10.33 per kilometer, respectively. Jefferson County is the home of Pine Bluff. With its 65,000 residents, it is by far the most densely populated city in this region, and it produced the most loan candidates. Outside of Pine Bluff, any given area could produce few candidates for loans. The other areas were comprised of tiny towns with depressed economies, which meant that such towns provided only small, low-income markets for anybody with a product or service to sell. "It has to be a losing battle over time," one loan officer asserted. "After you have made three or four loans, you have used up all the possibilities."

Those populations were (and continue to be) small in rural Arkansas because so many people had left. When opportunities decreased, much of the able-bodied population migrated to the North, where new opportunities exist. Age distributions in these counties showed a hollowing out between the ages of twenty and fifty, the age range in which most people are likely to start businesses. Many of the kinds of people who are likely to start business—those with the most entrepreneurial capacity—are also the most likely to leave those communities; in some measure, they leave behind the old, the less well educated, and the less able.

In addition to the low population density, there are differences in the nature of American markets, particularly in the size of production units and distribution networks for commonly used products. Much of the Bangladesh economy is characterized by small and highly localized markets. In that setting, it takes little capital to insert oneself into the system; it is possible to provide products, rather than services; and it is not necessary to be part of a national or even statewide production or distribution system. Hence, Grameen Bank can make loans to an individual to purchase a cow so that he or she can sell milk to the neighbors or to purchase a paddy-husking machine that also serves others in the immediate surroundings. When I lived in India, there was a little shop outside my house that sold individual cigarettes. If I wanted to purchase a pack, I would have put him out of business for the day. Under circumstances such as those, entry costs are low, and the amount of return required to provide some kind of living is small.

In the United States, by contrast, there are international, national, and statewide markets. Products such as milk are available in supermarkets or grocery stores, and the amount of capital needed to enter a production and distribution network is likely to be substantially larger. Any micro-enterprise loan fund with small amounts of capital available will find itself serving local needs; in the United States this means mainly providing services rather than goods, particularly the kinds of services not easily connected to a national or even statewide distribution system.

Even when successful, the Good Faith Fund mainly increased the quality of life of the working poor and those with moderate incomes rather than the really poor. This may be a laudable goal, but it probably should be classified as poverty alleviation rather than economic development.

Development can be defined variously, but somewhere in most of the definitions is the creation of additional wealth for a region. Development sets in motion a process of wealth-generating activities by increasing productivity, exporting goods, or substituting exported goods for ones made internally.

In the context of the total dollar value of the economies of even these poor local regions, the dollar investments are minuscule. But let us assume the programs made one hundred loans a year instead of twenty-five, and that all of these loans produced successful businesses. If most of the money went to produce basic services for a local population, there would not be very much in the way of net change. The day-care center operators, the beauty shop owners, and the dressmakers supported by the Good Faith Fund undoubtedly produced better incomes for themselves and provided convenient services for others; we can even argue that, by working in their homes, they became good role models for their children and others in the community. But they did not generate new money or provide additional employment opportunities.

Even the key success story described above, that of Beatrice Newsome's dry cleaning business, was not necessarily a story of economic development. She probably took business away from other dry cleaners, perhaps including her former employer. If that is the case, there was no net gain for Pine Bluff. One might argue that, if all the other dry cleaning shops were owned by whites, she, as an African American business owner, at least helped keep money in the black community and improved the economic balance between the races. But economies represent intricate sets of relationships. In Pine Bluff, it would also have been true that, if she undermined the white dry cleaners, she was also liable to put the black people who worked for her competitors out of their jobs. In any event, it is difficult to argue that any of these micro-enterprise activities in these communities represented a serious net gain for the community.

Because so many businesses are neither localized nor labor intensive, they require more than $800 or $900 to get started. Small amounts of capital thus do not go very far in helping those who want to start up a business in the United States. It is important to note here that I am limiting my comments to micro-enterprise loan funds, not to development-oriented loan funds in general. Indeed, I think there is an important role for loan funds that make substantially larger loans to real businesses with development potential, as did the other companies in Southern.

One can see, then, that the obstacles to generating volume for peer-group micro-loans to the really poor in a rural setting are quite formidable and that, without volume, the possibility of self-sufficiency for the agency is only a dream. The annual operating budget of the Good Faith Fund was in the neighborhood of $420,000, quite typical for an organization of this sort. Assuming no cost to the Good Faith Fund for borrowing money for their program and loans paying interest of 15 percent, one would have to lend out $2,800,000 per year—which, at $1,000 per loan, would have required a total of twenty-eight hundred loans. Of course, the organization could not come close to that loan volume, with a small staff. Of the seven micro-enterprise loan funds studied by Edgcom, Klein, and Clark (1996), none of the group-based ones averaged even a hundred loans a year. Their total average loan portfolios, excluding their first-year activities, as well as those of the funds that did not do peer-group lending, averaged out to about $275,000 per year. The Good Faith Fund was at that time close to the average.

One can try to reduce the costs of making these loans. An organization in New England called Working Capital does this by using preexisting groups and organizations to make the loans and supervise the process (Jeffery Ashe, personal communication). The other choice is to add new products and programs, which might have the result of producing more income and, incidentally, attacking poverty with a broader array of tools. The Good Faith Fund was very creative in doing so. The first element it added was a loan program to larger companies that, for one reason or another, were also underserved by the conventional banking industry.

In so doing, it emulated the strategy of its parent corporation, the Arkansas Enterprise Group. Their loans were between $25,000 and $150,000. Besides providing opportunity for business growth and development as well as income for the Good Faith Fund, the loans had the consequence of "normalizing" the Good Faith Fund in the eyes of the business community, which had tended to see it either as a charming little byway in the world of serious business or as something a little strange. For example, after the owner of an important Pine Bluff restaurant and bakery had his loan request turned down by the banks, he completely rebuilt his restaurant with the help of a loan from the Good Faith Fund. During the reconstruction process, he put up the standard sign announcing the project, which listed the architect, the contractor, and the lender—in this case, the Good Faith Fund. This is an excellent example of providing credit for economic growth to somebody who was unable to get it through normal credit markets. But the large loan made to this restaurant owner was some distance from a micro-loan made to a poor person for a marginal business.

The Good Faith Fund also introduced a new initiative, however, that provided assistance to low-income people. This was a job-training program that initially trained people for the health care industry and placed them in jobs. Subsequently, it became involved in other work-readiness training. The health care program was enriched beyond normal minimum requirements and worked to place graduates in quality health care establishments. For a while, the program hoped to earn its own way with state contracts, as welfare reform got underway. By maintaining high standards in both training and placement, the aim was to upgrade health care in southern Arkansas as well.

POVERTY AND ITS MEANINGS

A third difficulty in translating the Grameen model to the United States is raised by the difference in what it means to be poor in the United States versus in Bangladesh. To put it simply, the floor is higher in the United States (or Europe) than it is in Bangladesh. There, people starve frequently. In the United States, even when poverty is quite severe by our standards, having the opportunity to earn (only) a little more cash by starting some kind of business can be perceived by many as not worth the risk or effort. That can also be illustrated by other kinds of non-entrepreneurial examples.

We can ask the question in other venues about what steps people are willing to take to get some sort of income. We know that there are a number of jobs that Americans are loath to undertake. We have already discussed one of the major examples of that, the processing of chickens. In Bangladesh, the efforts required to be successful are likely to produce quite measurable benefits for individuals and their families; they will be noticeably better off. It is not at all clear that the efforts required to be successful in Pine Bluff, Arkansas, improve borrowers' lives quite as noticeably, and the individuals whose lives are improved frequently have other supports, as explained in the next section. This reduces people's motivation to take a loan to try to start a business, and it even reduces the motivation to pay it back. Taking a loan to start a business is a demanding and difficult choice for many people. At the same time, failure to return a loan is not a big deal if one does not want to get another. If that loan and its renewal stood between the individual and starvation, it would be paid off. Otherwise it can be perceived as a windfall, something like winning the lottery.

There is another issue that is related to where poor people stand in their society. To be poor in Bangladesh is to be part of a very large group; that is, it is commonplace, or normal, to be poor. In the United States, to be poor is to be out on a tail of the distribution; it is a relatively rare event related to special conditions. For example, in some small southern towns, it has been in the best interests of local elites to keep people poor (see Cobb 1992, 253 ff). In those circumstances, where a small elite controls the welfare system and access to any opportunities that there are, routes to achievement at the local level are closed down. In many of these towns cotton or other seasonal crops are important sources of income. If people have other full-time, year-round job opportunities, the costs of this seasonal labor will go up. Indeed, historically, the South, in general, invested relatively little in education because to do so would ultimately undermine the low-wage structure that the wealthy perceived was necessary for them to maintain their positions. In that kind of setting, local elites are unlikely to support programs that encourage independence and opportunity for the low-income people in their communities. In addition, there is the problem alluded to previously—that the poor who are left behind in rural America tend to be the ones who have limitations based on age, education, or ability, or the ones who have responsibility for large families or a family member with a disability. Consequently, they are also unlikely to be the people who undertake entrepreneurship opportunities.

THE SAFETY NET

Finally, the success of the Grameen Bank's program—or, more accurately, the limited success in the Good Faith Fund's peer-group lending program—is tied to the safety net available to participants and the conditions under which they are willing to relinquish that safety net. Although there are, in fact, some poor single mothers who have moved from welfare into employment, that was not true for any of the respondents in my sample. Instead, as is the case for many other loan funds, the recipients of these loans came from what might be termed either the working poor or slightly better off than that. All of the women were married and their husbands were employed, although often at low-income jobs. The women themselves had usually held jobs, as well. For example, one woman had been in the police department and was retired on disability; another had been a school bus driver working split shifts at low pay; still another had worked for a dry cleaner before starting her own cleaning establishment. Their husbands tended to be laborers, prison guards, GED teachers, and the like. The few men in the sample who were borrowers had wives who were also wage earners.

This, then, was mainly a hard-working group of two-earner, African American families in which the "business" supported by the Good Faith Fund was a second income or, in some cases, even a third. Their Good Faith Fund–supported income may have been smaller than that from the first job, but it combined to provide a more comfortable life. It was a source of supplementary income that was likely to be larger than other sources available, or it may have provided the opportunity for a mother to be at home with her children. In very few of these cases did husband and wife enter into a business by giving up both jobs. A more common strategy was to combine a secure income, on the one hand, with a more risky business venture, on the other—as if to balance risk or to ensure against failure.

Another aspect of this "safety net" was the constraints set by the welfare system. During the period of this study, there were limits to the assets one was permitted to have in order to keep benefits. If one purchased an expensive sewing machine in order to become a dressmaker, one now had an asset that reduced welfare benefits. Leases in public and subsidized housing also prohibited people from running a business in the home. It was a difficult choice to give up medical benefits to undertake the risky task of trying to make money by selling something. Those who know how these welfare rules work could add further examples of disincentives to this list. The point is that the success stories came from families who had a safety net of some kind: at least one secure source of income, along with the knowledge that taking this risk would not reduce the family's benefits; and, to carry the point from the previous section, an understanding that the hard work was likely to increase the household income and comfort.

This was in distinct contrast to the Grameen participants, who explicitly had no resources or safety net. I emphasize that this is not an argument favoring the disassembling of the safety net in this country. Rather, I want to suggest that micro-lending will not help those who rely heavily on a societal safety net. In this country, micro-lending is most likely to help those who are already in a position to take some minimal risks, i.e., those whose families already have at least one moderately secure income. Useful as this is, it leaves unaddressed the problems faced by those who do not have even such modest security.

By the mid-1990s, group lending had all but disappeared, and the Good Faith Fund had transformed itself into a job-training and employ-ment-readiness program. With a budget of more than $2 million, includ-ing new funds coming from state and federal programs to assist in the transition from traditional welfare to the new Temporary Assistance to Needy Families program, it trained workers for the health industry and gave others employment skills. This period was the absolute high point for the Good Faith Fund. It also had little or nothing to do with lending.

Micro-credit programs for so-called micro-enterprises have a role to play among economically depressed populations. But it is not a very large role. They work best with those who have well-defined skills and histories of holding jobs, rather than with those who are long-term welfare recipi-ents. When Good Faith Fund borrowers succeeded, it was because they were members of low- to moderate-income families, where somebody already had a job, and the Good Faith Fund micro-business loans pro-vided additional or supplemental income. Understanding that and target-ing this population appropriately would have made the funds more successful in generating loan volume, and in making people's lives better and moving them toward self-sufficiency.

If programs like these are going to have a larger impact in terms of creating opportunities for more poor people, they will have to define themselves as connecting individuals to the labor force in multiple ways. The promising early success of the health care training program of the Good Faith Fund and the employment counseling program of a well-known fund in Chicago suggest that programs providing job training ser-vices, in addition to offering loans, are crucial for reaching the numbers of people necessary to have an impact. The expanded nature of these pro-grams allowed them to become more than boutiques for a few people.

Finally, group process is unlikely to be a useful tool in the United States for generating repayment or continued participation unless the group had a long-term prior basis for being in existence and meaningful social ties among its members. Individuals who are relative strangers and who have no real stake in each other's success (or failure) are ineffective as a peer pressure group, although they may provide some support and other types of assistance for each other. Even then, it is possible that rural programs will have additional difficulty because of low population density and, concomitantly, small markets. It is possible that such programs will be more effective in urban settings. In both cases, though, it may be chimerical to expect group processes to work the way they do in rural Bangladesh.

Solutions to dealing with the problems of the poor in this country follow fads and trends. And there is some desire to find "one-size-fits-all" solutions. The courageous experiment of the Good Faith Fund reminds us that even seemingly similar local conditions across a variety of settings do not actually call for the same solutions without a great deal of adjustment. It reminds us that there is no magic bullet for solving the problems of the poor. A whole array of approaches is probably desirable, with each approach making a modest contribution to the outcome.

Nevertheless, it is important to point out that this discussion takes place after ten years of a worthwhile effort. At the time that the Good Faith Fund was established, programs like it in the United States were relatively rare; but among those who knew about them, there was much excitement about their potential. It took imagination and courage to start a program in a new place and to do so de novo. Under the circumstances, it was worth a try. One should count it as an important experiment that was not nearly as effective as hoped. On the scale of other efforts to deal with poverty, it was not a very expensive effort either.

Opportunity Lands

The one company not explicitly aimed at making loans in the Southern organization was Opportunity Lands. Modeled to some extent on the City Lands Corporation, which was a subsidiary of the South Shore Bank holding company, its job was to invest in property and upgrade it. Unlike the other companies, whose goals made it possible to find entrepreneurs wherever they might be whether or not it was a good idea from a development point of view to do so, the Opportunity Lands effort, because it was rooted in real estate, was, by definition, place-based. But unlike the Chicago company, whose primary mission was to upgrade dilapidated housing generated by weakened markets during the racial change process, the Arkansas company's initial focus was to build incubators—facilities where small businesses could share services, such as clerical and electronic, as a way of reducing overhead costs.

City Lands' focus on housing had made sense in Chicago's South Shore community because the area was dotted by large, multiple-family dwellings that years of neglect had turned into slums in their neighbor-hoods. So visible were these neglected structures that, without the capac-ity to turn these buildings around, Shorebank would not be able to encourage private efforts at real estate improvement. Blocks with these large, under-maintained, and ugly buildings, with their boarded-up win-dows and weedy wisps of grass, would swamp the efforts of smaller-scale, individual investors trying to upgrade their own buildings. And, there-fore, they would not make the effort. Each investment, then, in these buildings had a major positive impact on the surrounding area, as those improvements encouraged smaller stakeholders in the area to upgrade their properties.

In addition, this activity was fueled by the large federal housing sub-sidy programs, such as Section 8 Rehabilitation, which made such enter-prises economically viable. Investment in business activity in South Shore, in general, was not as central as investment in housing because the neigh-borhood was mainly a residential area, with many of its residents working in downtown Chicago or surrounding areas. Although those interested in doing development had to pay attention to deteriorating shopping strips there as well, the promotion of business life and the economic opportuni-ties it provided were not central to the community's economic vitality.

By contrast, in southern Arkansas, with the exception of Hot Springs, large multiple-family residences were virtually nonexistent in these target towns, although each had its pockets of subsidized housing with high-density housing arrangements. Even more important than that, the Southern Development Bancorporation had determined that business growth was its goal—the road for improving the southern Arkansas economy. Initially, then, housing development did not figure centrally into the process.

The first manager of Opportunity Lands came to Arkadelphia from Baltimore, where she had worked on economic development activities. Her first task was to supervise the renovation of the headquarters for Southern in space that was part of the Elk Horn Bank building; the second was to find appropriate, incubator-like, development projects. She found a building that had housed a large, but now out-of-business, furniture company. Situated on one of the main streets of town, the empty storefront contributed to the run-down look of the area. Renovation of that building had one desired effect: to transform the look of that part of town. Instead of empty, large, plate-glass windows framed by wood molding with peel-ing brown paint, the building became an attractive, single-story office facility with airy rooms, light colors, nice windows, plantings, and pretty signage. There can be little doubt that this effort slowed or ended the decline of Arkadelphia's downtown and was an important early step in what became, over the next eight years, a steady trickle in downtown building and business improvement.

Ultimately the Enterprise Center had a mate across the street; and elsewhere in town, the community's other major bank constructed a dramatic new facility that it chose to build in town instead of out on Pine Street, where much of the business growth was taking place. All of this business activity in the downtown area contributed to the appearance of vitality in the community. The renovation of the space for Southern was a great success. The offices, with their cool, industrial grays, gave off an aura of business-like elegance somewhat different from the more common bank/lawyer offices in Arkadelphia, with their heavy, dark furniture. The building also gave off an aura of great prosperity, which belied the fact that, in some respects, the whole Southern operation was under-funded.

The problem was that Opportunity Lands used up almost of all its cash to create the Enterprise Center, and its management had nowhere to turn next. The Enterprise Center did not earn money to pay for itself, nor did it produce profits that might have attracted a buyer. During the tenure of the first manager, it was never rented up, and there was no take-out strategy to provide resources for the next endeavor. It was difficult to find resources for a second project. Serious attention was given to finding government support to renovate an old hotel building, which was also downtown, and to convert in into senior citizens' housing. There seemed to be state and federal programs that would have provided subsidies for this effort, but, if there were, they were never landed. This may have been another case where it was difficult for outsiders to gain traction with local officials. Before a subsidy could be found, the hotel burned down. Consequently, Opportunity Lands existed as a developer, but with no resources to do development. It was not long after this that the first manager was replaced by an Arkansan who had experience in real estate both in government and in the private-for-profit sector.

Her first task was to rent up the lovely Enterprise Center building in order to cover operating costs and debt service. To do so required an aggressive marketing campaign for tenants. The effort was successful and the building was occupied by an array of renters; however, few of them by themselves could be considered business development. For a time, AEG occupied about 25 percent of the building's space. With its own receptionist and office staff, AEG's separateness from the rest of Southern was intensified. Professionals, such as lawyers and accountants, were prime tenants, as well as not-for-profits, such as the Main Street Program, designed by government to encourage downtown development activity. As money became tighter, AEG moved in with the rest of Southern. Although the building paid for itself, it neither made money for the company nor found a purchaser.

From the perspective of doing development, the story is obviously more complicated. On the one hand, the building created an environment for the downtown area—what economists call an externality, which made it more attractive for other business activities. On the other hand, it never really became a successful incubator.

A similar project was undertaken in Pine Bluff on Main Street. If Arkadelphia's main shopping district looked tired before the arrival of Southern, Pine Bluff's looked totally desolate. At that time, Pine Bluff's original downtown area was quite large, with Main Street stretching for fifteen blocks. As is the case with many small towns and cities, virtually all shopping activity had moved out to the mall on the outskirts of town— this one anchored by a WalMart and a Dillard's department store. Consequently, almost all fifteen blocks displayed strings of totally empty storefronts. The devastation was heightened by the fact that Pine Bluff itself was (and is) very poor. Two small nodes of activity broke up the desolation. At one end, down around First Street, were the buildings that housed the functions of government—county and city offices with their attendant courthouse. Further south, up around Eighth Street, was the post office along with a newly constructed museum, a tool in the city's plan for downtown revitalization. A few viable shops, such as an office supply store, clung to the edges there.

Although there were compelling reasons to purchase that building —the property was available at a good price and the title was relatively free and clear; the building was relatively young and in good shape— Opportunity Lands chose to locate its Enterprise Center somewhere in the middle, at the place where train tracks ran through town and in a no-man's-land between those two more successful nodes. A better strategy would have been to work out from one of the more successful nodes, therefore consolidating an area that was more or less working or had some promise. In contrast to its counterpart in Arkadelphia, the Enterprise Center in Pine Bluff had little impact on anything around it. For some time, the Good Faith Fund was its prime tenant, with other spaces taken up mainly by not-for-profits. For example, the local Small Business Development Center had its office there.

It became clear to management that the incubator strategy was not likely to be very fruitful. Vacancy rates were high in these towns, and rents were very low. Potential entrepreneurs could get all the space they needed at very low prices. True, the old spaces were not likely to be wired for modern uses, but neither did the entrepreneurial energy available require it. In addition, these centers did not pay for themselves, and there was little capital available to pay for new investments.

Consequently, following the model of its Chicago cousin, Opportunity Lands entered into the low-income housing business. There had been a half-hearted attempt in Arkadelphia to team up with a local developer to build small, single-family homes under a program similar to Section 8. Small, inexpensive houses would be made available for purchase with little or no down payment and with monthly mortgage payments to be no more than a third of income—the government paying the difference between the actual mortgage cost and the owner's payment. That enterprise did not make progress. On the other hand, Opportunity Lands' second manager, who had been an official in state government, began to demonstrate that she knew how to arrange for subsidies for low-income housing.

From a financial point of view, one of the major virtues of constructing low-income housing is that governments—city, state, and federal—could put up much of the money and provide guarantees for mortgages. This meant that the developer did not have to have much of his or her own capital. After construction was complete, payments could come out of the income stream from rentals. Using this strategy, Opportunity Lands, with almost no capital of its own, was able to get four projects underway. The first started in an impressive and promising fashion. In Pine Bluff, Opportunity Lands purchased twenty units of severely dilapidated low-income housing and three vacant lots from the Resolution Trust Company. The properties were all located on a block close on the edge of the city's downtown area. The plan was to rehabilitate the buildings and construct new ones on the vacant lots, and then to put them back on the market as low-income rental housing. The city of Pine Bluff cooperated in the program, providing a second, forgivable mortgage (made available by a statewide housing program), and also helped to find other financing in town. The plan initially appeared to be a stunning success. Upon their completion, the houses on Chestnut Street were transformed. Still of frame construction, they were spiffily lined up on both sides of the street in delicate pastel colors. The street looked like a model block in a model community in small-town America. The beauty of the block impressed the government of Pine Bluff, local citizens, and also employees of the Good Faith Fund, who were then the only full-time employees of Southern living in Pine Bluff. For Good Faith Fund employees and, perhaps, for others, the effort represented a concrete result from company activities and a project in which they could take pride.

At about the same time, the company purchased twenty-five lots in Clarendon, Arkansas, for the construction of affordable homes. The original plan called for financial assistance, from HUD and Farmers' Home Administration, that would result in a market price of about $37,500 for each. Efforts were made to find builders with innovative systems to provide methods for the construction of innovative low-cost housing. Products that looked promising did not live up to their promotions, and those houses were never built.

Heartened by the initial Pine Bluff effort and again supported by the city, Opportunity Lands started a second low-income housing project in the city. It purchased a formerly lovely, old, craftsman-style apartment building near the Chestnut Street houses, but also close to one of the nicest areas in that part of the city. After a period of neglect, it had caught fire and had become a large and visible eyesore. Despite Opportunity Lands' apparent success with Chestnut Street and various city and state guarantees, no bank in Pine Bluff at that time would provide a mortgage for the project, and the company had to turn to an Arkadelphia Bank to provide funding. Putting these deals together was no easy matter.

Upon its completion, one of the Opportunity Lands' employees in Arkadelphia moved into the building as resident property manager. It was then that unforgiving reality struck. It turned out to be surprisingly difficult to keep both the apartment building and the Chestnut Street Housing rented up and maintained. Tenants were being evicted either for not paying rent or for destructive behavior.

Visible deterioration of the Chestnut Street houses was rapid and dramatic. The mini-blinds in the windows went first. Property management could not keep up with the decline. At one point, Opportunity Lands hired an off-duty policeman to function as a part-time security guard. But it was not too long before the units began to resemble their former state. Aggressive eviction of destructive tenants or those who were delinquent payers meant that there was some difficulty keeping the buildings at the level of occupancy required to maintain a positive cash flow.

Similar problems surfaced in the apartment building, but in a more dramatic way because there were more units. It was difficult to get some tenants to pay rent. The company employee responsible for renting up the building, collecting rent, and maintaining order was seriously threatened with physical harm. The building became a site of persistent difficulties and another money loser. The most positive financial result was that Southern received tax credits for the renovation of a historic landmark.

Clearly, the task of maintaining low-income rental housing was not easy. Indeed, at this time Shorebank and other developers around the United Sates were having difficulties too. This was a time when urban areas felt like lawless places, hit both by crack cocaine and very high levels of unemployment.

Subsidies like that one were important for all of Opportunity Lands' efforts. For example, in the deal of the Chestnut Street houses, there was a $22,218 low-income tax credit, which would be good annually for ten years. Similarly, some of the financing from a community development block grant—$143,000 worth—was scheduled to be forgiven at the rate of 10 percent a year for ten years.

With what initially appeared to be a successful start in Pine Bluff, Opportunity Lands also undertook low-income housing construction in Helena, Arkansas, a city on the Mississippi River and about 150 miles east of Arkadelphia. As I pointed out in chapter 1, Governor Clinton had invited the Shorebank Corporation to come Arkansas because of the intractable poverty in the Delta region—that is, in the old cotton-growing and former plantation areas along the Mississippi. But the company was unable to find a satisfactory bank at a reasonable price to purchase there. There continued to be a sense, both on Southern's board and among some of the supporting foundations, that to be a success, Southern would have to make some impact in the Delta. In some sense, locating the Good Faith Fund in Pine Bluff was a response to that concern. Although not quite in the Delta itself, Pine Bluff had been the gateway city for the southeast corner of the state, which is also part of the Delta. Helena, then, became another entry point into the "real" Delta. Indeed, at the beginning of its interest in Arkansas, Shorebank in Chicago employed one of its minority, former employees to spend time meeting with officials and activists in order to see if he could find a basis for intervention there. In addition to Opportunity Lands' efforts, the Good Faith Fund operated an office in Helena for two years with one loan officer, and for a time even AMS had a representative sharing that office.

With still some of the charm and faded ambience of a river front town in the old South, and once a place of some prosperity, Helena then had a poverty rate of around 30 percent and an unemployment rate in the high teens. Its battered main street still had the look of an old-fashioned, country town, and residents had the hope it could be revived and become a tourist attraction, if only the financing could be found. The city of Helena had undertaken three big development efforts with its own leadership. A slack water harbor on the Mississippi as well as a riverfront park were constructed there. There was, as well, a modern attempt at an old-fashioned riverfront marketplace; a charming museum, which focused on the history of the Delta; and, trying to capitalize on its own history, the King Biscuit Blues Festival, which brings fifty thousand people into the city each autumn for a weekend of blues. As one might guess, local shopkeepers try to gain, as well, from such an effort by selling music and related materials. And some of the grand old houses in the area have been converted to bed and breakfast inns, trying to capitalize both on the festival and the evocation of an earlier lifestyle in grand old dwellings.

Aside from the high levels of unemployment and poverty that characterize the town and some serious distance between the races, there are two other important aspects of Helena's development activities that should be mentioned. The first is that one of few bridges in the area that crosses the Mississippi River is approached through Helena. Normally, that might be seen as a positive. However, immediately on the other side is the Lady Luck Casino, a large gambling establishment with both a restaurant and the capacity to sell alcohol. (Helena dealt with the restrictions on alcohol consumption characteristic of Arkansas's many dry counties by having "private clubs.") Although the casino is a sponsor of the Blues Festival, it has drawn business away from the few moderately successful downtown restaurants, which ultimately closed.

The second fact about Helena is that, at least for whites in the middle class and higher, things are under tight control, following a tradition that has characterized Delta towns for more than a hundred years. One personal experience illustrates just how tightly things are run. I wished to conduct a survey in Helena and, because it was so far from Arkadelphia, I tried to find a local collaborator. I looked up the social scientists at Phillips County Community College. I found a sociologist and phoned him, asking if he would like to undertake the task. He responded positively, but then never returned another call. I then phoned another appropriate person. She also agreed to conduct the survey, but subsequently returned no calls. In frustration, I turned to the president of the Winthrop Rockefeller Foundation and asked for his advice. He put me in touch with the county's state representative, who also operated a major oil company franchise in the county. We had a pleasant meeting, and I left him my questionnaire. Two weeks later the phone rang in my office. "Hello, my name is Regina Harper (fictitious name), and I have been assigned to be your research assistant by the president of Phillips County Community College."

My interpretation of what happened is that my first two contacts were instructed to ignore my request. When somebody who was a known and important person intervened to make the request, the president reversed his decision. Ms. Harper subsequently proved to be a wonderful assistant in a difficult task.

That survey produced additional evidence of the seriousness of Helena's problems. A few survey questions comparing the results in Helena to the results in Arkadelphia are illustrative of that fact.

TABLE 5.1: PERCENTAGE RESPONDING TO, ARE THINGS GETTING BETTER OR WORSE IN YOUR COMMUNITY? IN HELENA, ARKANSAS, AND ARKADELPHIA, ARKANSAS

	HELENA	ARKADELPHIA
Worse (%)	64.8	20.8
No change (%)	21.4	37.7
Better (%)	9.7	40.3
Don't know (%)	4.1	1.2

TABLE 5.2: PERCENTAGE RESPONDING TO, WHICH OF THE FOLLOWING CHARACTERIZE YOUR COMMUNITY? IN HELENA, ARKANSAS, AND ARKADELPHIA, ARKANSAS

	HELENA	ARKADELPHIA
Leaders work for the community (%)	21.9	54.7
Leaders work for themselves (%)	40.3	28.9
Leaders fight (%)	23.5	3.8
No leaders (%)	11.6	8.2
Don't know (%)	2.7	4.4

It was into this area that Opportunity Lands entered with a plan to provide upgraded poor people's housing in a renovated multi-family frame building across from a grand old church and in a series of newly constructed smaller units. It was in Helena that things finally really fell apart for the company. Part of the problem was the tyranny of distance. Opportunity Lands attempted these projects operating from the head-quarters in Arkadelphia. The 150-mile trip took three hours by car. And its manager tried to work with local minority contractors who, in many cases, did not have a long track record. The result was a quagmire—inadequate financial controls led to a situation in which some subcontractors got paid too much and others did not get paid at all. Similarly, some unsupervised subcontractors did such shoddy work that buildings began to fall apart before they were completed.

This led to a company crisis. The manager of Opportunity Lands in charge of this project left, and it took some time and approximately $1 million for the company to dig itself out. There were a number of issues involved in this disappointing result. But it is clear, as we have seen before, that there were high costs that resulted from the pressure on the company to produce in ways that would satisfy particular constituencies. One result is that resources were spread too thinly, making it even more difficult to be effective. And, as in the case of Pine Bluff, there was limited success in the effort to connect to local groups in a way that would augment the thin staffing and supervision that this Southern subsidiary had available to provide. Both the Good Faith Fund and AMS faced similar problems in this setting.

The Elk Horn Bank

After the first president of the Elk Horn Bank had resigned, Shorebank sent one of its executives to be interim chief executive officer until a replacement could be found. After eight months, he left for health reasons and was replaced To fill in the gap, the Shorebank Company sent its best Chicago lender to Arkadelphia to manage things. During the first interim period, Shorebank conducted a vigorous search for a permanent president, looking for one who was already working in Arkansas. Several suitable individuals were identified as candidates for the job, but they either wanted rates of compensation that were excessive or they wanted to make arrangements so that they would not have to live in Arkadelphia.

So Shorebank then sent the original interim manager back to Arkansas for a short term which stretched to seven years. Although he was officially president and CEO of the whole Southern operation, he, in fact, did not have authority over the mangers of the other divisions, who still reported to Chicago. A talented manager and someone who came to be well-liked in the community, he was never able to pull the disparate parts of the organization together. If we refer back to the discussion in chapter 2 of the organization's beginnings and to Max Weber's description of specially loaded dice that, with each roll, increase the probability that the numbers will turn up again, relations among the units of Southern were, by now, so firmly in place that they were not easy to change. To some extent, the existing company managers saw no need to accept the new president's leadership.

The Elk Horn Bank was a relatively smooth-running operation. It had high standing among bank examiners and other ratings systems, such as Sheshunoff, a well-known bank-rating and data-collecting company. It also had a group of loan officers in place who were experienced and who had high standing in the community. In my experience of interviewing borrowers, I was often struck by the positive feelings people expressed about this older group, as well as stories they could tell about long histories of relationships. These loan officers followed the procedures of traditional southern bankers, emphasizing personal relationships over technical evaluations and being loath to change the standards by which they made loans. However, one of the innovations that Shorebank brought to the Elk Horn Bank was to put bank lending on a more businesslike basis, so that its constituency could be expanded beyond those kinds of personal ties. But to do so required the collection of much more information—resulting in a new layer of bureaucratic requirements and procedures. This effort to put lending on a more businesslike basis had costs. People who had gotten their loans because of personal relationships were offended when they were subsequently asked to fill out new forms. One man said, "I have been banking there for twenty-five years and I never missed a payment. Now they're treating me as if I were some (#*&#!*) foreigner from New York!"

Much of the bank management's efforts were devoted to operating a successful bank in a highly competitive environment. During this management phase, two bank branches were opened: one out near the interstate in an adjoining town where business activity was growing and the other in the growing town of Bismark, midway between Arkadelphia and Hot Springs. Another branch was substantially renovated. During much of this time, bank advertising also had to counter the advertisements of the other large bank in town that emphasized it was a local establishment run by local people. Nonetheless, several pieces were put in place to try to move the bank in a development direction.

The first effort was to get the bank identified as a "preferred Small Business Administration lender." Like southern banks in general, the SBA was also more conservative in its loan guarantee practices here than it was in the North. The interim Shorebank manager sent to help run the bank had been a former SBA official himself and had worked with the SBA to make its procedures more comparable. The advantage of becoming a certified SBA lender was that it greatly speeded up the turnaround time in the decision-making process.

Over time, four new lenders were hired. One had been a lending official for a federal farm loan agency and had also grown up in the area. The other three were a white man from southern Arkansas who had graduated from a famous Ivy League school, something he felt the need to tell people he encountered and who left Southern to work for Shorebank in Poland; a black woman of Jamaican ancestry from New York, who was also a graduate of an elite northeastern college; and a white man from Monticello, a town near Pine Bluff, who had recently graduated from business college and whose primary responsibility would be development lending. This last person had the least difficulty connecting to local clients. Like the people at AMS and the Good Faith Fund, the three non-local officers struggled to boost loan volume. This was an even more difficult task for the black woman, part of whose job it was to find minority borrowers.

Much of Elk Horn's banking activity was of the traditional sort. Those in the timber business made up a large part of the local economy and were important customers of the bank. One might find a local garage owner needing money to upgrade his machinery. A bigger customer had a thriving business in Malvern that produced timber trusses for roofs and that later branched out into housing construction.

A great deal of what the bank considered development lending continued to be most successful in Clark County and had a substantial impact on Arkadelphia. A bowling alley was opened by a young couple who had been unable to find funding elsewhere. A franchise of a mainstream national motel chain opened out near Interstate 30. A greeting card and gift store received money for expansion, and a few other shops downtown were funded as well. With its new agricultural expert, the bank had a large impact on the development of the growing local poultry business.

Each year the bank did extensive lending, both as a standard community bank and as a development bank. In averaging the three years from 1991 through 1993, for example, total lending came to approximately $26 million a year. Development lending in those years came to about 20 percent of that total. Development lending was compiling a good track record. For example, in 1993, charge-offs were only $34,000. Between the period when Southern decided to purchase the bank and the year's end in 1996, deposits grew from $47 million to $92 million.

A bank president in a small community is not merely a faceless operator of a company. He is expected to get out into the community to attend booster-type meetings, such as Rotary, and to be on a first-name basis with customers and local residents. This Southern official did particularly well in this regard. Watching him greeting people at the Clark County Fair, for example, was to watch a person connected to the community.

If the Southern mission had been to improve the economy of Clark County instead of all of south Arkansas, it would have been labeled a success. Closely following the hopes of the first Elk Horn Bank president after it was purchased by Southern, the majority of its loans were made in the immediate area. By 1997, the county was doing well. Its unemployment rate had shrunk from approximately 13 percent to 3.7 percent, putting it among the lowest in the state. In 1987, its economy was ranked forty-fourth of sixty-eight Arkansas counties in per capita income. By 1997, it ranked thirty-fifth (Condit 1997). This was not only Southern's achievement. As we shall discuss in chapter 7, the achievement was part of a larger community effort in which Southern was one of the pieces.

However, its management could claim substantial concrete accomplishments. This included the $56.5 million in development loans and investments into the South Arkansas economy. Through that activity, they could claim that they participated in creating and sustaining more than twenty-six hundred jobs through the end of 1995. In addition, it was one of the top Small Business Administration lenders in the state and a Lender of the Year in 1996. Its lending activity was important in the development of the poultry business in Hot Spring and Clark counties when other local banks were reluctant to enter this field.

Although it was slow to do so, Southern was able to convert the Good Faith Fund into a successful job training program in the medical services area. Opportunity Lands did produce one hundred units of housing for low-income people and three enterprise centers, two of which had an important impact on their community.

None of these achievements is trivial, particularly when accomplished in a poor state whose residents were not particularly welcoming. Southern's staff was energetic, imaginative, and devoted to its task. Nonetheless, there were numerous ways it might have been more effective in achieving its stated goals. As we shall discuss it chapter 7, those claims in many cases confuse outputs with outcomes.

CHAPTER 6

Local Management Takes Over

Ultimately, the Chicago company's management services were terminated and, although company officials offered to provide assistance if necessary, their continuing relationship ended. The CEO of Southern left Arkansas and returned to Shorebank as chief financial officer, and the Southern board took more direct responsibility for running the company. The story of the transition is instructive, for it points to the ways in which local elites are able to maintain their dominant power in a region.

First, a look at some of the events that led to this transition. Forced by pressure on its own resources and expansion of its activities elsewhere, the Shorebank Company had proposed to the Southern board that it purchase Southern and make it a full-fledged subsidiary of the Chicago company, instead of continuing the relationship with a management contract. For several reasons, this proposal was rejected.

The Arkansas board was feeling some discontent with the progress of Southern. Furthermore, the representative of the Walton Family Foundation who was an advisor to the board reported that the head of the Walton-owned banks had been watching the financials of Elk Horn and was not happy with how the bank was being managed. In his judgment, although the bank had high ratings from the federal bank examiners and Sheshunoff, it was not sufficiently profitable. According to his report, they were particularly dissatisfied with the bond portfolio. (It should be noted that an outside agency evaluating that same portfolio gave it high marks.) This came as something of a surprise. He was therefore strongly opposed to the merger.

While the board was debating what to do, the managers of Southern —all of whom had been hired by the Shorebank Company—compiled a report in which they suggested that a merger with the Chicago company would not be particularly advantageous and, indeed, might have negative consequences.

After a year of deliberation that included the option of retaining the then-current CEO (an offer that was declined), the board of Southern made the decision that it would be best for local management to take charge of the company. The board also came up with a new chief executive officer. He was the president and part-owner of a bank in the desperately poor city of Helena as well as an important official of a national banking organization. In the face of grumbling from the board about the return on equity and assets of the Elk Horn Bank, it was surprising to learn that the new CEO's bank had similar, or worse, performance by almost every measure.

By raising capital from foundations, including the Walton Family Foundation, the Southern Development Bancorporation purchased the Helena Bank. As a consequence, this executive and other well-established families in the Helena community realized significant profits. The two top-ranking African Americans in the Arkadelphia branch of the bank either left or were fired, and, according to knowledgeable sources, pressure was substantially reduced for the Elk Horn Bank to make development loans. The very successful second manager of the Good Faith Fund was also let go. The company subsequently purchased two other Delta banks located in Mississippi.

In chapter 4, I discussed the fact that there were always two legal constraints of quite different weight for bankers engaging in development lending. The first concerned the possibility of lawsuits over lending liability when lenders gave development advice to borrowers. The second was concern about Section 23A in banking legislation. The original Southern management was relatively unconcerned about the first, and staff at AMS and Southern Ventures very often became quite involved in managing customers' companies. Upon stepping in to take control, the new CEO expressed such concern about potential lender liability problems that the AEG manager proposed that the only way to avoid the threat entirely was to stop giving technical assistance. On the matter of Section 23A, the old Southern management had followed the regulations scrupulously, but they also saw to it that the bank played an important development role. Returning to the old pattern of traditional southern banks, the new management used fear of lender liability to reduce the role of the bank as a development lender. Under the new model, according to people connected to the lending function, the spur to do development bank lending was generally reduced, with AEG (renamed Southern Financial Partners) now taking the lead with a program to receive grants from the banks in order both to operate and to make loans.

What can be called development lending is always a question. There are always ways to increase the scope of what development loans might be called. For example, the former CEO and owner of the Helena Bank thought that his bank had always been a development bank, although it had not been an SBA lender. Whatever his efforts at development, Helena remained dreadfully poor.

Yet, what is also true is that new management now had the opportunity to have a larger impact than its predecessor. As discussed previously, Arkansans seemed uneasy about outsiders from the start. As one of the investors explained it, "We are really a closed community. It is not something to be proud of, but it is true." A consequence of this was that support from state government agencies, teamwork with other banks, and general broad-scale support for the original Southern program was generally not forthcoming. With the shift in ownership and with the organization being run by insiders, that pattern had clearly changed. The organization now had the opportunity to leverage resources in important new ways and to increase the probability of its effectiveness. To the extent that there was a continued commitment for development activity, the organization had the capacity to achieve at a whole new level.

Under the new management, procedures were tightened up and control was centralized. Everybody reported to the chief executive officer, and there were no independent bases of power. The open quality of the operation also changed. At least one person who was let go, for example, was made to sign a document agreeing not to say anything about the company to outsiders. Loan quality was much more tightly evaluated than it had been in the past, and the whole operation became more bureaucratized. The service area of the new company was greatly augmented, and loans were more widely dispersed than ever. Whether or not the additional bank branches reduced the consequence of diffuse activity is yet unknown. The challenge is still to distinguish true economic development from making an array of unconnected loans.

My story of the Southern Development Bancorporation actually ends with the change of management. But, at the moment of transition, the new management had clearly inherited an institution with an organizational structure that they could never have built by themselves. Both the vision and the resources that the Chicagoans had brought to Arkansas in the creation of Southern were impressive. The new group had the advantages of local ties and the lessons learned from the previous effort. One can only hope that the idealism and commitment that infused the original program, supported by substantial investments by local and national foundations and government resources, will inform the company's future. Doing development in Arkansas is no easy task. Were it so, it would have been accomplished some time ago.

CHAPTER 7

What Can Be Learned?

Any discussion of the lessons learned from this enterprise should begin with some humility and also with admiration for all of the players who risked resources and their own reputations to take on a task both audacious and daunting. Understanding much of what did not work well is the product of hindsight; and many of the obstacles encountered in the process that may seem obvious when looking backward were not to be anticipated. Simply to take two of the items we began with—efforts to purchase a bank and the choice of a board—it is clear that the consequences of both sets of decisions probably were not in anybody's calculations. Similarly, the magnitude of the initial achievements—raising more than $12 million, purchasing a bank, and putting in place a complex organization staffed by talented people—is, by itself, a tremendous accomplishment and easy to take for granted. In some of my own writing, I characterized the enterprise as the construction of a great multi-masted ship, sails unfurled, sitting in a harbor. Inevitably, one wants to see what it can do.

It is also important to bear in mind that this enterprise was conceived as an experiment. Nobody knew for sure what might happen. One thoughtful program officer at the Winthrop Rockefeller Foundation asked plaintively, on one occasion, "What happened to the idea that this was an experiment with lots of unknown parameters, and opportunities to learn? It is now being perceived as a business that is expected automatically to succeed, and people are unreasonably impatient with false starts and errors. This is about learning."

That is an important point. But once that big ship is standing there with all the resources it took to build, expectations change. Pressures mounted to get moving, to make lots of loans, to tell good stories, to become economically self-sufficient. We saw how, even at the beginning, the Southern board was becoming impatient at the slow process of finding a bank. In addition, investors wanted good stories, and the company obliged by providing them. The Good Faith Fund was featured on national television when it had almost no achievements commensurate with its budget and aspirations, and those aspirations were confused with the achievement. "Poster children" were picked to provide the heart-warming stories that a thirsty set of stakeholders and the public required. It is with that context in mind that I turn to thinking about useful lessons from the Southern Development Bancorporation's history.

The first point is that every development project has to be sensitive to local context. Each setting brings a new set of issues that may not be easily anticipated, and, once encountered, must be confronted. In the case of southern Arkansas, the local context included extreme localism and hostility to outsiders. The depth of that reality was never perceived either by the Arkansas leaders who invited Shorebank to the state or by the Shorebankers themselves. To the extent that it was recognized through the first years, it was met with a shrug, as if this were a small problem that would go away. But, while things improved for some knowledgeable residents in Arkadelphia, the problem was slow in dwindling—partly because the style of Southern managers kept reminding local residents that these people did not belong, and partly because, for many, the fact that they were from Chicago settled the matter. It took a long time for Southern to understand that it needed bridge builders who, in fact, could carry information both ways. Similarly, Southern was slow to employ local people in key positions and to make use of their abilities. It would be easy to castigate Southern for this slowness. But there are, in fact, good reasons not to rush in. For example, if problems in the structure and values of the community are part of the reason for an economic lag, it may be a mistake to hire local people who are so deeply embedded in their community that they share the same standards. In some instances, even if the local people do not share these standards, they may be subject to peculiarly local pressures from those for whom development, particularly as it focuses on the more depressed sections of the community, is not to be desired. Nonetheless, each local employee brings with him or her large networks of personal contacts and understandings that may facilitate desirable outcomes. But it takes time to learn the lay of the land and to know how to limit the constraints and take advantage of the gains presented by hiring local people. Southern did, in fact, move in a more local direction in its hiring, and it began to make use of local talent in a new way. To the extent that these local people had real power, some of these matters improved.

Creating Leverage

For those in banking and the world of finance, the idea of leverage is an obvious one. The original conception is that of a lever, which, if properly situated, can multiply an individual's capacity to move objects. As applied to finance, this lever was first understood to be the sophisticated use of credit, such as purchasing stocks on margin to generate additional resources. The generalization of that model was to use small sums of money to generate much larger ones. This might be done by using small sums to bring in numerous other players; to open the flood gates of subsidy; to make resources grow quickly; or to have the expertise to make it possible for one to be a partner to others with cash resources. A perfect example from Shorebank in Chicago would be the way in which the undercapitalized City Lands Company became an equal partner with First Chicago Corporation and RESCORP to do the $25 million deal on the Parkways redevelopment, a rehabilitation project in South Shore covering nine square blocks. Not only were the capital resources of First Chicago and RESCORP put to use, but, in addition, a whole panoply of federal and state subsidies, as well as the syndication of passive tax losses and the sale of tax exempt bonds, were put into play.

Although Southern seemed well capitalized compared to Shorebank in its early years, as I have discussed above, the dollars actually available were totally inadequate to the task when compared to the size of local economies. Under those circumstances, it was essential to make those dollars do multiple duty. The activities in the first years of Southern seemed, by some standard, to be remarkably unleveraged. In the first years, as others also pointed out, Southern often acted alone, without investment partners. In a review of Southern Ventures' performance after a series of setbacks, one board member commented that he thought one function of the company was to bring many other players to the table; in reviewing the Southern Ventures' portfolio, he was surprised by how little had been done in that regard.

The loan portfolios of Elk Horn Bank and AMS also seemed remarkably unleveraged in this sense. In the early years, Opportunity Lands had faced the same problem. However, as the company moved to a low-income housing strategy, it was able to make use of state and federal funds for its programs and to get some of the financing it needed from other banks. These newer projects did represent leverage at work, as they both multiplied resources and brought local bankers into some aspect of the development process. Housing rehab projects can also provide jobs and some additional cash flow into their communities. They can illustrate visibly that something real is happening, and, in some particularly dispirited places, they may provide a kind of encouragement. Having a tangible accomplishment around which to mobilize support for more comprehensive efforts may be very important. AMS was able to augment its lending resources through the use of federal funds as well. But it was less able to partner with state and local agencies.

The Elk Horn Bank should have been a model of leverage itself. Purchased for around $5 million, its assets approached almost $100 million by 1998. However, it fell victim to the myth of a self-sustaining organization. With AMS, Southern Ventures, and the Good Faith Fund all in need of resources, the bank was under pressure to be vastly profitable so that it could help support those organizations. Consequently, it was forced to put aside plans to augment its staff, which would have allowed it to do increased development lending.

By extending the metaphor, there is another way to think about leverage. Not only must one expand monetary resources to gain power, one must also expand people resources. Southern was a small organization. For it to achieve its goals, it needed to activate and mobilize the energies of many others who were spread over a broad region. Because it perceived itself mainly as a credit agency, it did not initially see the need to mobilize lots of other players. One of the great advantages of Southern being taken over by a group of local Arkansas managers after 1996 was that it was easy for the new management to find partners and to take advantage of the consequent leverage. In this, they have been especially successful.

With its creation, Southern Development Bancorporation set for itself an unusually high standard for a relatively small, private development project: the transformation of the economy of a region. It could, for example, have chosen simply to make the lives of some poor people better through credit or counseling or both. That is a much simpler standard. If that had been the goal, it would already have produced a substantial achievement. In its first five-year period, it lent out or invested about $125 million (of which $19.5 million was defined as development loans) to 180 small business customers. In any model of success, a measure, such as the number of loans made or the number of jobs created by those loans, would always have been an important proximate goal. Nonetheless, the enterprise was characterized by numerous disappointments. The collapse of Southern Ventures, the technical assistance difficulties and high loan losses of AMS, and the failure of the Good Faith Fund to live up to its aspirations and hype reflected, in part, the failure of Southern to connect in effective ways to its surroundings. As I will discuss below, more modest goals might have produced superior long-term outcomes.

What Does It Mean to Do Development?

A question seldom faced by organizations that accept "economic development" as their mission is, What does it really mean to do development? To many in the development business, this sounds like mere academic nit-picking. In answer to that question, people have shown me new housing in low-income communities and waved their arms around with pride and a sense that the answer was obvious. Counting loans, even those defined as development loans, is not an adequate answer either. There is a difference between measuring outputs instead of outcomes. There has to be some way to demonstrate that net income has changed for a group of people or that the people in the region have changed and, with that, the pattern of opportunities. Without that, all one does is move resources among the same group of people. In addition, a concomitant of the idea of development is that opportunities will improve specifically for low-income people. Yet, it can be demonstrated that most so-called development programs benefit those who already control substantial resources, such as real estate (Molotch and Logan 1987).

In terms of merely moving the money around, economists use the term "substitution effects" to describe how some gains can be canceled out by losses elsewhere, or the ways in which inputs might be found if they were not initially provided. A good illustration of how that works or might have worked is the story of the dry cleaner in Pine Bluff discussed in chapter 5. She said quite explicitly in her interview that her initial Good Faith Fund loan was "no big deal." She could have assembled the same money from her credit cards or from relatives. We could imagine, then, that, as an energetic and resourceful person, she would have gotten launched one way or another—that is, she could have substituted one set of resources for another. Similarly, as I have pointed out already, it is not clear that her efforts represented a net gain in any way for Pine Bluff. If we had searched diligently, we probably would have found some other dry-cleaners who were newly hurting. This case suggests an important way in which people who try to do development often over-represent their achievements. Having created an audacious and brilliantly conceived plan that took seriously the notion that credit and capital could be a driving force in real economic development, and having set itself the goal of a real net change in the economy of a particular region, Southern did not always behave as if the economic development of a geographical location was its goal, or as if the gains should go to existing residents, including the poorer segment of the population. There were some good reasons for this that I will discuss below—which include pressures from foundations and the need to earn money on development efforts. Nonetheless, with widely and very thinly spread lending activity, it is difficult to see how much in the way of real development could occur under Southern's program.

One of the sources of pressure to generate loan volume, no matter where or how, came from the expectation that the mechanisms to achieve that goal would be self-sustaining—that is, that much of the program could be made to pay for itself. This is a particular problem for some foundations which would like to start the process going and then move on to the latest thing. Setting this as a standard had the consequence of further setting constraints on what might be achieved. However, like the ancient and continued dream of a perpetual-motion machine, such self-sufficiency is probably not achievable. The more appropriate challenge might be to define honestly what is the level of continuing subsidy that makes the enterprise worth the effort, rather than to constrain the task even further by trying to make it pay for itself.

The other consequence of being forced to be self-sufficient is that other means to generate business growth get slighted. This could include anything from sophisticated technical assistance to changing people's sense of what options were available to them. If impact on the economy of a region is the goal, some redeployment of effort will be required. Local economies involve large numbers of dollars and numerous actors. The question is whether one can find the tools that will pry open the economy and move it to new levels. Economies do not move consistently and in the same way across all dimensions. The task is to locate the points at which pressure will effectively move things to a higher level.

In South Shore, for example, the most dramatically successful impact of Shorebank came through its focus on the real estate market. Efforts at encouraging small businesses never really succeeded. The second part of the problem was that Southern was operating with relatively limited resources. Capitalized at $12 million or $13 million, its largest single asset was a bank that came to have $100 million to deploy and various subsidiaries with around $8 million at their command. Calculating the total dollar value of any local economy is a very difficult task. But the numbers are very large. For example, total income for Clark County, Arkansas—a county with a population of 21,437—was $277.6 million in 1990. The construction and equipping there of one new factory branch of a major company in 1992 represented a cost of $100 million. What this meant for Southern was that it needed to multiply the effectiveness of its resources, a serious "loaves and fishes" problem. I have already discussed the issue of leverage as one way of dealing with the problem. The need for people and organizational leverage was augmented by the fact that it takes more than loans to alter economies, if they are alterable at all. Lots of players have to be mobilized to undertake many different tasks. The hope is that, if movement begins to occur, others will see that movement and take action to hop on board. Again, returning to the Shorebank analogy in Chicago, we saw that, if somebody fixed up some of the large and most deteriorated buildings, many private individuals became motivated to improve their buildings too; independent actors in large numbers beyond the direct impact of the South Shore Bank and the City Lands Corporation joined in the process of making change. In addition, then, to the processes of bridging and leveraging to achieve that result, two more related matters should be identified: focus and synergy. Although these were understood by Southern to be part of its repertoire, there were so many other pressures on the organization that the Southern companies often failed to optimize these orientations. I turn to each of these issues next.

FOCUS/TARGETING

The metaphor here is the use of a magnifying glass to focus the sun's rays. Left to themselves, these rays are spread around diffusely enough to provide light and energy; but only when properly brought together and aimed can they start a fire.

In its literature and strategic planning, focusing or targeting had been a guiding rule for the Shorebank Corporation. As Southern began to be organized, it became clear that some effort had to be made to locate an area in which to target activities. Southern Arkansas is an area of more than twenty thousand square miles, with a population of 650,000. It was clear that an organization without substantial resources could have no impact at all.

As I have discussed, Southern did give lip service to targeting, but very quickly—partly under the pressure of generating loans and invest-ments in volume and mostly because of limited staff size—targeting dropped by the wayside. If, on the one hand, net change was to be used as the measure of success, the size of area to be targeted was a problem at best. The smaller the target area, the easier it is to have an impact. But if, on the other hand, loan volume was the measure of success, the small target area, at least in the early stages, was a problem. In addition, it would have been difficult to raise large amounts of money for a small area with a small population. When the residents of Clark County and the president of the Elk Horn Bank expressed disappointment that the development program of Southern was not to be focused exclusively on them, one of the Shorebank officials asked, "Who would give us $13 million to develop only Clark County?"

Yet, as the target got bigger and wider, there was also the problem of coordinating activities among the group of companies. For most of its life, AMS had two or three lenders, one of them being its manager, and one or two technical assistance providers. Southern Ventures spent most its years with two investment officers, one of whom was the manager. At some point, an additional person was hired to provide technical assistance. Opportunity Lands had two or three people in the office, one of whom was primarily clerical. Although the bank had more lenders than that, only three were defined as development lenders; the others primarily serviced their traditional clientele, and, in some cases, after a lifetime of making traditional loans, they had difficulty with the concept of development lending. Only the Good Faith Fund, far away in Pine Bluff, had a staff size consistent with its aspirations, including, at times, five or six lenders. The number of permutations possible among six towns and five companies with somewhat different agendas is dizzying. When it became clear that targeting was not happening because there were simply too many towns, there was talk of emphasizing different towns in the group on a rotating, year-by-year basis.

In addition to the pressure for loan volume, there were other centrifugal forces that forced the spread of meager resources. First, pressures to do more work in the Delta persisted. As discussed previously, these pressures led to housing development in Helena with poor consequences, and to a small, shared branch office of AEG and the Good Faith Fund that had few accomplishments. Second, there was growing sentiment to do minority deals wherever they could be found—particularly since Arkadelphia had only a small minority population and because almost no minority deals were being done there.

Finally, there was pressure from the venture capital company, Southern Ventures, to broaden its base of operations. As previously argued, the logic of a venture capital company requires a broad and diverse portfolio, with a key assumption in the development of this portfolio being that most of the companies included will fail, but that those losses will be made up for by a few big winners. It is necessary, then, to find a reasonably large number of promising young or start-up companies. From the venture capital company perspective, the problem of limiting deals to a few target cities or counties is that, in a region with a weak economy, a sufficient number of deals to make the system work cannot be found. In addition to business deals in Hot Springs, Malvern, Arkadelphia, and Pine Bluff, Southern had deals in Paragould, Heber Springs, Little Rock, Benton, and Springdale—that is, in locations all over the state. One should add that the venture capital company had pressure from potential governmental partners, such as the Arkansas Development Finance Authority, to commit itself to further statewide activity. As I have discussed, spreading out activity reduces the possibility of actually contributing to development. It also makes the problem of judging good borrowers and tracking their performance more difficult.

Competition versus Cooperation

At one point early in Southern's history there was one other kind of discourse that led away from the companies focusing their activities on a particular area, and that relates to the problem of organizational coordination. The divisions of Southern were a loose confederation. In my interviews with managers, they often discussed their efforts and programs in terms of "my company" instead of the organization as a whole. There was nobody strong enough to make them act as one. This was so much the case that, at one point, one of the Shorebank managers argued that excess concern about coordination would lead to delay and to passing the buck, as clear lines of individual responsibility would be vitiated. This was an era when the idea of entrepreneurial management was in vogue, and the idea was that aggressive and competitive managers would be more likely to achieve if the pressure was on them to do so. Where there are five companies, each being run by an entrepreneurial type, the argument goes, the individuals will work very aggressively to make a record. If coordinated efforts are required, each entrepreneur will wait for the other, and each then has an excuse for not delivering—that is, blaming the others for his or her failures. By shifting the responsibility from individual leaders to collective effort, the force of entrepreneurial drive is blunted.

This is a classic problem in management. To the extent that the individualistic orientation is adhered to, coordination is difficult. Yet, too much reliance on group process weakens the drive of individuals and may lead to the creation of cumbersome bureaucratic procedures. The problem is that such a model works for some organizational types and not for others. Where resources are slender and the tasks are large, it makes sense to be concerned about augmenting resources by cooperation rather than encouraging independent entrepreneurs to follow activities down different and unconnected roads. Management tried to change that model when they observed the consequences of such independent efforts, and the lack of organizational coordination that ensued, by bringing in a consultant to work on team building. But by then it was too late. Southern's new local management perceived that problem in the organization's history when they took over at the end of 1996, and they subsequently moved to far more centralized control. By then, there was no longer any notion that AEG, now renamed Southern Financial Partners, was a separate company, and, in its new organizational structure, all divisions were directed to report to the new CEO.

Building Synergy

It should be clear by now that lending, by itself, is not going to make economic development happen. Many players have to be on board: political leaders, important business people, and the heads of important local institutions. Effective community leadership may assist in the development process. Community leaders can help get funds to revitalize main streets or train leaders. They can mobilize the population to vote for new resources. They can generate enthusiasm for innovation. They can vigorously assess the resources they have and try to discern how to build on them. And they can effectively do other things, such as recruit branch plants and attract political attention to their region. Of all the towns studied in this project, Arkadelphia was unusual in its level of leadership. It was the one community we surveyed in which the majority of the respondents said that leaders worked for the community, as compared to working for themselves, fighting with each other, or simply being absent.

To begin with, community leadership supported the sale of the Elk Horn Bank to the Chicago group. This was in contrast to some other communities, where fear of losing power to outsiders trumped trying out an economic plan to upgrade the community. As the man who sold the bank said, "We thought we had done all we could. It was worth a try." Arkadelphia's community leaders had raised the money to build a new hospital that attracted doctors, and this hospital had evolved into being a medical center for much of the region. They built the industrial park and, when it failed to attract new businesses, they persuaded Clark County citizens to vote on a tax, the proceeds of which went to install the sewage system that prospective renters decreed they had to have. And they kept their word with citizens by repealing the tax after the system was built. They built a "spec" (speculative) building to attract new businesses to that area. When emergency funding was required for the industrial park, a local family foundation put up the money. That foundation also put up money for a lecture series and musical performances as part of the process of getting the two colleges in town to work together. Serious resources were invested in the high school. Other members of the community started a metal-working network that did group purchasing, lobbying, and apprenticeship training.

During the time of this study, from 1988 to1997, community leaders were working with the two colleges to explore the possibility of making Arkadelphia an attractive retirement community. The thought was that, with the two colleges there, an array of cultural activities might serve as an attraction. There was even talk of allowing the sale of alcohol if that were essential to make the program work. There was a concerted effort to make the community more attractive to modestly affluent, retired people. It could be argued that it was just such effective community leadership that supported the sale of the Elk Horn Bank to the Southern Development Bancorporation. In some other communities, fearful that they would lose control of their local bank, leaders discouraged similar sale proposals. The point is that development is very hard to do anywhere, but especially so in settings where local leaders fear its impact will result in a loss of their power. To make development work, numerous individuals and organizations have to be involved in the process. Where many other things are happening, providing credit becomes a facilitator, as others try to fit themselves into the process. The best analogy may be that using credit as the lead tool is something like pushing a wet noodle from behind.

Tangentially related to the use of local capacities is the role of race in making loans and generating minority business. To set the standard of "manufacturing" or "import substitution" for minority loans in this setting is a problem for anyone, but perhaps even more so for African Americans. Most of the black middle class consisted of school teachers, agents of the state bureaucracy, and people who had jobs in national companies. African American small business options included beauty salons, gift shops, mortuaries (a product of segregation), and small restaurants. One of the most successful African American customers of Southern was a man who produced personalized pens, napkins, badges, and the like for weddings, church events, and fraternal orders. To encourage African American businesses in this setting required a special set of goals. In addition, there was the problem of lending across race. Most of the loans made to African

Americans in Arkansas by Southern were made by other African Americans. That had not been true in Chicago's South Shore, where race seemed to play less of a role in lending than it did in Arkansas. Indeed, Shorebank's most successful lender to African Americans was white.

The story in Southern was quite different. Very few loans were made across races in the white-to-black direction. Southern Ventures did not do minority deals until the African American on the staff nominated herself to be a specialist in minority affairs. At the Elk Horn Bank, the new, young minority loan officer, mentioned in chapter 5, made most of the minority loans there. Trust, communication, and commitment all seemed to be salient issues. Minority borrowers appeared to be more comfortable with minority lenders. Where borrower and lender were the same race, communication was better between them than when they were of different races, particularly if there were large cultural differences between lenders and borrowers. Given the nature of minority entrepreneurship in Arkansas, minority deals were harder to find and harder to structure than other kinds. Minority lenders with a strong commitment to making that type of loan may have been more willing than the average white lender to construct a deal. One African American respondent speaking in another context pointed out that, in some ways, at least one aspect of race relations was better in 1953 than it is in the present. As she put it, "At least, then, you knew that prejudice and racism were out there, and, when you ran into difficulty, you knew why. Now that it is more concealed, one never knows for sure why difficulties occur."

Let me provide one example. A young African American woman who worked on my project went to the local automobile dealer to purchase her first car. She was told that she could only purchase the smallest and cheapest car that General Motors made—and that, at list price. Much of the driving in the area is on the Interstate highway, and, besides, this woman had a family. Such a car was inappropriate, and her salary was such that, by conventional guidelines, she should have qualified for a loan to purchase a larger car. She felt frustrated, as if something were not quite right, but she did not perceive this as a consequence of her race. I suggested that she go to the Elk Horn Bank for a loan, and I interceded on her behalf. The development loan officer at Elk Horn said that the car she wanted was well within the parameters of her income situation, and he made the loan. But he went even further. He phoned the automobile dealer, according to his report, and said, "Stop fucking with that little girl. She's family." When she returned to the dealership, she was treated very differently. She got the car she wanted, and she was offered a better deal on the price. It was only then that she was sure that race had played a role in her previous negotiations. Not a negligible person, she is today a high-ranking administrator in the Arkadelphia school system.

Closely related to that story is an issue of priorities. If the economic goal is defined as developing a region and there are limited staff resources to do so, energy would be better spent on bigger and easier deals. Those loans will have larger consequences and the dollar volume will be larger, giving the organization making the loans the opportunity to make strong claims about achievement. The assumption is that, as the economy improves, so will the position of minorities. By contrast, if one defines the goal as helping minorities take a seat at the table, the effort of working closely with minorities takes on a new kind of priority. The minority lenders at Southern defined their role as the latter, although one or two of their superiors did not always share their zeal.

Another part of that challenge is to face the reality that making loans to small businesses may decrease the number of workers required and therefore reduce employment. In the short term, that seems not to be effective if one is looking to help low-income people. One of Shorebank's other subsidiaries once posted a chart that showed increases in loans used to buy machinery and subsequent declines in employment. One hopes that, if greater wealth is generated, business will increase, providing new employment opportunities down the road.

Problems with Technical Assistance

The leverage issue also plays an important role in thinking about technical assistance. How does one effectively deliver technical assistance at varying levels in a way that is more effective than one-on-one? We have seen how AMS tried to do other things, such as sell a bookkeeping program and advice about marketing. This was because part of AMS's original mandate was to deliver technical assistance to promising small companies. Providing technical assistance is always difficult, as I suggested in chapter 4. But if one had local partners and knew how to work with them, the cost of technical assistance would be dramatically reduced. I have already discussed the development organizations that were created to do just that in communities. Southern's rejection of the offer to help by one local business school is an example of refusing to externalize a costly aspect of the development process.

Externalizing the technical assistance function becomes even more important if an organization is forced to become self-sustaining but has inadequate income to achieve that difficult, if not impossible, goal. I have also suggested that networks, as purchasing groups, might be able to select people they approve of who provide industry-specific, rather than generic, guidance. Such groups are also a good example of a way to provide specialized technical assistance in wholesale fashion, and they also exemplify the effective use of leverage.

An alternative solution is one used in Finland. There, companies select their consultants, who are paid for by a government agency. If the clients like the results, they agree to pay the consultant themselves down the road. This program has the consequence of companies hiring consultants they respect and to whom they are likely to listen, and it is qualitatively different from the response of entrepreneurs to people presenting themselves as generic "experts."

Supply versus Demand

The underlying model of Southern started with the assumption that local businesses and people who wanted to start businesses were starved for credit. Once Southern announced that credit was available, it was believed that people would stand in line to receive it. Clearly, that model was simplistic and inaccurate. Few people presented themselves with bankable deals to any of the financing subsidiaries. And that persisted as a problem. Under what conditions might it have changed?

One could imagine a situation in which people did not think of using credit to start or expand businesses because none was available. It might be that, as people observed others growing or starting businesses, they would be encouraged to try. In addition, it is possible that economic growth in one place would generate growth in others. In Stuttgart, Arkansas, for example, the growth of a Lennox Air Conditioning manufacturing unit led a local entrepreneur to start a company providing pallets and other wooden platforms for shipping equipment. One could imagine a situation in which a growing managerial class would have increased need for yard and garden services, as another example. Nonetheless, the true story is that there was not a lot of demand for viable loans, and, during these first years, the availability of credit did not generate a need for new credit.

The question, then, is how to generate demand? The Good Faith Fund was probably the most effective company at taking the show on the road, generating publicity for itself, and trying to find audiences to target. Nonetheless, the generation of demand still needs more attention as a development issue. Generating demand was part of AMS's original charge, but one that did not receive much attention from the company. It is not clear that anybody has really figured out how to generate such demand yet, although, in recent years, it has certainly gained a higher priority as a development problem. In the early years of Southern there was talk of a business plan contest, although that program died aborning. Within Southern's so-called target area, there was (and is) an array of business schools—Henderson, Ouachita, University of Arkansas in Pine Bluff, and Phillips County Community College, all of which have business programs of some sort. Those schools primarily teach people how to function effectively in the corporate world. They do not do much to encourage entrepreneurship. One could think of courses that could play that role. And one could think of events such as "entrepreneurship nights," in which successful business people come to talk about how they did it, which might be effective.

Identifying Catalyzing Activities

If focus and leverage are present, new sorts of energies should be released. Once the pot is boiling, lots of things are taking place simultaneously, and people discover new ways to work together to achieve shared ends. In these circumstances, even people not directly involved in the process define the community as a place where things are happening, and they have a chance to climb aboard. Community groups mobilize to demand political resources, and their demands seem viable because a reasonable base of activity has been established. This was the context as Southern's companies began to discover new ways to assemble their shared resources—one small example of this being the rehabilitation of a house by Opportunity Lands using outside bank funds so that a Good Faith Fund customer could establish her business in her home. Similarly, the Enterprise Centers in Arkadelphia contributed mightily to the revitalization of the city's downtown. Making the area busier and more attractive had the consequence of numerous other independent actors beginning to play a role. New small businesses came to town. Others spruced up their properties. A competing bank began a major reconstruction of its property, and numerous new businesses opened up there. This did not happen only because of the efforts of Southern; other groups in the community also took action, which contributed to the improvement of Arkadelphia's economy. Synergy also happened when community leaders called on Southern companies with proposals for deals they could assemble using political resources. And, finally, the ultimate sign of synergy was when citizens began to devise new ways to tackle old problems for themselves, because they felt increasingly empowered and effective.

HIDDEN CATALYSTS

The frustrating thing about trying to measure development impact is that one can influence outcomes even by one's presence and not necessarily know about it. One story illustrates this vividly. One of the Southern companies wanted to make a loan in one of the Delta counties to an African American who wished to establish his own funeral home. Although, normally, funeral homes are segregated, it was not the case in this town, where the white-owned establishment hired this man to deal with African Americans. He rightly saw that there was a market for his own establishment.

Just before the loan was closed, the lender discovered that the borrower already had a loan from a funeral home society that was highly disadvantageous. The terms of the previous loan included a statement that the lender (the funeral home society) had the right to determine when a borrower was delinquent and, if he was so deemed, he would have no further right of appeal. The lender would then be able to take over the funeral home, which was the collateral. Under those circumstances, Southern did not want to do the deal. But it offered to take over the funeral home loan at a slightly advantageous rate of interest. Much to everyone's astonishment and sense of frustration, the borrower rejected the deal.

Several months later, I met an attorney from that town and, in the exchange of pleasantries, I told him about my interest in Southern. "What a wonderful company," he exclaimed. "I have a client, whom Southern helped immensely." Since it was not a very large town, we were able to figure out quite quickly (with appropriate guarded discourse, since attorneys are not supposed to talk about their clients and I was not supposed to talk about bank customers) that his client was the African American mortician. "But he did not do the deal!" I blurted. "Yes," he said. "But he took those terms to the funeral home society and was able to get a still better deal."

In a situation where there is monopoly lending, a state of affairs often faced by African Americans (often also historically true for purchasing life insurance), the lender can set his own terms. In the sudden face of competition, that situation changes dramatically. How much this kind of hidden catalyst takes place, bringing new energy and new opportunities into a community, is something we will never fully know.

Were it not for the accidental fact that I bumped into this attorney, neither I nor anybody else connected with the Southern enterprise would have ever learned about this story. In efforts to understand levels of achievement, this kind of important result goes uncounted. Worse yet, if one is supposed to earn money while at the same time "doing good," this counts against Southern. That organization's employee probably spent at least a week trying to make this deal work, and it was close to a three-hour drive from Arkadelphia to the man's town. But the economic return on her effort ultimately went to other people's bottom lines.

Adequate Resources

Other important issues to be considered are providing resources appropriate to the problem, setting a time frame that confronts the magnitude of the task, and resisting the impulse to make the organization becoming self-funding. We have already seen that the resources for this enterprise—given the magnitude of the problem—were pitifully small. A real estate development company that used up its capital in the first deal, a venture capital company with enough money to do approximately ten or twelve investments, and a lending company that was forced to push up its volume in excessively risky ways so that it could generate operating income were not in a position to do the job properly. Similarly, because these enterprises were forced to extend their reach beyond the capacity of a small staff to supervise activities, they, ironically, were forced to take actions that undermined their substantial achievements.

Understanding Requirements for the Job

As we have seen, Southern set out to hire the best possible people to manage its companies. All of them came with impressive records. However, in almost every case, their people skills did not match their keen intelligences. It is not clear how one might have known this in advance. Closer attention to the problem of bridging would have helped, since Southern's task required a huge investment in building relationships. Unfortunately, the demand that people work fast so that they could tell good stories to funders abridged the time available to build those ties. Although it would have required educating the funders to tolerate it, a higher priority might have been given to going slower and building the kind of personal and trusting relationships that would have helped sustain the work of doing development.

Conclusion

In short, regional economic development is always difficult to do. One may think he or she has a magic sword that will cut through the difficulties or the key that will suddenly unlock capacities. In regions that have lagged economically for generations—where both people and material resources have been siphoned away and market size and population density is low—the task is a complex and difficult one. Problems tend to nestle together. Lack of capital, poor health, low levels of education, willingness to settle for little or to give up, on the one hand, and exploitative systems where a few people, indeed, appear to benefit from the disadvantages of the poor and are consequently not highly motivated to do something about them, on the other, interlock in ways that perpetuate the problems. Southern's efforts to help unlock the capacities of the region through capital were admirable, and the organization's capacity to make loans for those trying to improve their position was impressive. A real program, however, to turn around the region's economy would have to focus further on the other sets of historically accumulated problems that a region mired in long-term poverty faces. Southern's new management, learning from the past and building on the achievement of the old, has been moving down that road. Whether its wheels will get stuck in the conservatism of traditional bankers or the protection of their pre-existing properties is yet to be seen. If the whole operation is seen as a continuing experiment, there will be much yet to be learned and the potential for impressive results. The danger is that the effort to present to the world a smooth show will undermine the possibility of learning, and it will end up being yet another way to maintain the status quo.

Methodological Appendix

The Research Approach

When Shorebank officials began to consider the Arkansas proposal, they approached me and asked if I would be willing to do both a kind of chronicle of their efforts and what came to be called a formative evaluation. That is, I would provide information about the process as a kind of feedback so that midcourse corrections might be made.

This was similar to the work I had done in Chicago's South Shore, where I conducted community surveys, interviewed the main actors in the Shorebank company on a regular basis, and attended public events. That set of procedures, then, became the model for my efforts in Arkansas.

Over the next eight years, my goal was to collect information in as close to real time as feasible. This was important because historic reconstruction often misses important forks in the road where one choice has consequences for the future. Understanding the road not taken often makes it possible to imagine other outcomes. But it also helps one to see that particular outcomes were not inevitable.

The most important method for this part of this process was the conducting of regular but informal interviews with the major actors in the company. I would try to meet with them on a monthly basis and discuss what was happening, what were their major achievements, problems, and plans. A few of the officers then took me under their wings and invited me to accompany them when they called on customers or prospects. Similarly, I met on a few occasions with directors and asked them how well they thought the company was doing and what changes or outcomes they would like to see.

I also talked with community members about their perceptions of the company's activities. I might learn things from them about which I would then ask company officials. For example, I heard the story of the dressmaker described in chapter 2 from two sources before I discussed it with the relevant Southern actors. These informal interviews sometimes took place in an office and other times over lunch.

From these officials I also collected company-produced internal documents, including annual reports and strategic plans. I attended meetings where issues, problems, and plans of Southern were discussed, as well as events—such as the first year party, which was also described in chapter 3. I attended Good Faith Fund borrower group meetings and the larger programs organized for a number of groups assembled together.

There were several efforts to collect systematic data as well. Because I was concerned to know how economic development issues impacted current residents rather than new people who might move into the community, I conducted random sample surveys on a door-to-door basis of four hundred respondents in each of what appeared to be the target communities. My goal was to collect information about what the communities were like before the Southern intervention and then to conduct reinterviews afterward. Ultimately, we conducted interviews in seven towns and follow-up interviews in four of them. The survey asked people about their residential history, their education and work histories, income data, expectations for their communities, what they thought about entrepreneurship, and similar pieces of information.

I also systematically surveyed a sample of customers of the various Southern companies, asking them about their efforts to find loans elsewhere, the nature of their experiences with Southern, and some details about their businesses, as well as their number of employees and annual revenue. As with the community surveys, I went back after a time to respondents and asked them how they were doing. This was very useful, because, although in some cases they were flourishing, in others they were already out of business or on the brink of being so. Often, by listening to their experiences, I could understand why. In one case, the company looked as if it were flourishing, partly because it was deploying its loan effectively. But a return visit two years later found this company sadly floundering. The hopes and plans that justified the loan never could be realized.

Over time, we collected other systematic information. Each of the Southern companies shared with us information about their loans. We also went to the communities where lending had taken place and collected information on bankruptcies and new business start-ups. We collected welfare and unemployment data as well as other indicators about the economic condition of the communities.

All of this activity was conducted out of an office on the campus of Henderson State University. I had one full-time employee, utilized some student workers from time to time, and hired door-to-door interviewers by word of mouth and from newspaper advertisements.

One added feature to this process was the South Arkansas Rural Development Seminar (SARDS). The purpose of SARDS was to marshall the skills of local scholars to think about development, to collect relevant

data, and to have a continuing dialogue about the Southern efforts. Arkadelphia had two colleges with social science faculty members. Southern
Arkansas University was in Magnolia, about seventy miles away. And
there was the University of Arkansas in Pine Bluff, as well as the University of Arkansas in Fayetteville. SARDS met once a month for five
years, with faculty members doing research projects that we discussed
along with other development issues.

We also considered the progress of Southern's efforts. Through this
seminar, I gained a sophisticated group of local scholars and collaborators
who could explain the world of South Arkansas to me. One of them
brought graduate students with him from time to time, and they also
worked on connected projects. Indeed, he also received two graduate students from Henderson State who decided to go on in sociology. They also
were able to produce some publishable papers. What was striking to me,
given the teaching loads and administrative responsibilities that this
group of faculty members carried, was that they accomplished a great deal
and attended our meetings faithfully. (The president of the one of the two
universities in town told me that he hoped their research interests would
not distract them from their real duties, teaching. This was a dramatic difference from my own institution, where research and publication came
first.) Every bit of activity in and with the community became useful information. For example, one of the SARDS team received a research grant
from a large northern organization, one of the few landed by members of
either institution. The local gossip was that she had received that grant
because she had been in an intimate relationship with me. Although this
was untrue, I came better to understand that other successes in the community ascribed to particularistic or unsavory connections might also not
be accurate.

All of these activities produced a rich array of information. But they
had their pitfalls as well. For example, my continued presence among
Southern officials was something of a problem. The old Shorebank group
had been long-term friends and acquaintances. Indeed, some were my former students. With them, I was quite relaxed and informal. The new
group of Southern managers did not share the same history, but I behaved
as if it did. I recall an event in which somebody was talking about her
Scrabble group. I commented that I was impressed that she had found
people with whom to play the game. "What are you going to put in your
book?" she asked. "That I spent my time partying and not working?"
Another member of the Southern team was dating a member of the
SARDS group. He complained bitterly about feeling that he was in a fish
bowl.

On the other hand, people used me as a message carrier to others. In these cases, I was not always as discreet as I should have been. On one occasion, a Southern employee told me she thought of quitting. That night at a dinner party, some of her superiors were praising her work. I suggested that if they liked her so much, they had better talk to her. She was, as she should have been, quite angry that I spilled the beans about her plans. Sometimes in disputes between organizational members I found myself taking sides.

The ambiguity of my position was such that I was even asked to serve on a Southern task force to plan for future activity. I did not know how to avoid participation, because I did not want to set myself apart from such normal congenial social processes. In cases such as these, instead of being the detached scholar, I simply became an involved participant, sometimes even taking sides.

Finally, the feedback generated by SARDS was not always welcome. The seminar group was quite shocked when the Good Faith Fund hired a group of whites to deliver Good Faith Fund products to their predominantly black clientele. I invited the Good Faith Fund director to discuss the matter with us. She brought with her a director of the company who told the SARDS seminar group in no uncertain terms that we should mind our own business. On another occasion, our group, reviewing the strategic plans of the various Southern affiliates, expressed surprise at how little each affiliate was working with the others or coordinating activities and their efforts. I brought this information to management, who explained that Southern was an entrepreneurial company and that this style was a way to encourage individual efforts and achievement. Coordinating efforts, therefore, might provide opportunities for each manager to blame the other, with the result that things would not get done in a timely manner.

In short, access to the management of Southern gave me great opportunities to achieve understanding of the processes, constraints, and motives under which people acted. Few research scholars ever get that kind of access. But, in retrospect, I came to realize that, just as others confused my roles, so did I, and that, in some circumstances, I did not achieve the detached standards that scholarship requires.

The final result was a treasure trove of information. The challenge, then, was to use it effectively to tell this story not simply as a narrative of events, but as a means of understanding the process of doing economic development and of learning from those observations the key problems in generating economic growth among the historically poor so that future efforts might have greater probability of success.

References

Aldrich, Howard E., and Catheline Zimmer. 1986. Entrepreneurship through Social Networks. In *The Art and Science of Entrepreneurship*, ed. Donald Sexton and Raymond Smilor, 3–23. New York: Ballinger.

Barnard, Chester. 1938. *The Functions of the Executive*. Cambridge, MA: Harvard University Press.

Bates, Timothy. 1993. *Banking on Black Enterprise: The Potential of Emerging Firms for Revitalizing Urban Economies*. Washington, DC: Joint Center for Political and Economic Studies.

Bellah, Robert, Richard Madsen, William Sullivan, Ann Swidler, and Steven Tipton. 1985. *Habits of the Heart*. Berkeley: University of California Press.

Bornstein, David. 1996. *The Price of a Dream: The Story of Grameen Bank and the Idea That Is Helping the Poor to Change Their Lives*. New York: Simon and Schuster.

Cobb, James. 1992. *The Most Southern Place on Earth: The Mississippi Delta and the Roots of Regional Identity*. New York: Oxford University Press.

Coleman, James. 1988. Social Capital in the Creation of Human Capital. *American Journal of Sociology* 94: 95–120.

Condit, Tom. 1997. Internal memo for the Ford Foundation, New York City.

Edgcom, Elaine, Joyce Klein, and Peggy Clark. 1996. *The Practice of Microenterprise in the U.S.: Strategies, Costs, and Effectiveness*. Washington, DC: Aspen Institute.

Eräheimo, Tapio, and Henri Laakso. 2000. Franchising-Entrepreneurship in Finland in Year 2000. Paper presented at the International Entrepreneurship in Finland Conference, Helsinki, Finland.

Festinger, Leon, Henry W. Riecken, and Stanley Schachter. 1958. *When Prophesy Fails*. Minneapolis: University of Minnesota Press.

Frank, Andre Gunder. 1979. *Dependent Accumulation and Underdevelopment*. New York: Monthly Review Press.

Hirschman, Albert. 1958. *The Strategy of Economic Development*. New Haven, CT: Yale University Press.

Kuznets, Simon. 1959. *Six Lectures on Economic Growth*. Glencoe, IL: Free Press.

Molotch, Harvey, and John Logan. 1987. *Urban Fortunes: The Political Economy of Place*. Berkeley: University of California Press.

Moy, Kirsten, and Alan Okagaki. 2001. *Changing Capital Markets and Their Implications for Community Development Finance*. Washington, DC: Brookings Institution.

Norton, Joseph Jude. n.d. Lender Liability, Law, and Litigation. Lexus-Nexus.

Pinsky, Mark. 2004. Personal communication from the president and CEO of the National Community Capital Association.

Pressman, Jeffrey, and Aaron Wildavsky. 1984. *Implementation: How Great Expectations in Washington Are Dashed in Oakland [CA]—Why It Is Amazing That Federal Programs Work at All*. Berkeley: University of California Press.

Reed, John Shelton. 1983. *Southerners: The Social Psychology of Sectionalism*. Chapel Hill: University of North Carolina Press.

Rostow, W. W. 1990. *The Stages of Economic Growth*. 3rd ed. New York: Cambridge University Press.

Santakallio, Esa. 1998. On the Development of Education in Technology and Entrepreneurship in Finland. Manuscript, Department of Teacher Education, University of Oulu, Finland.

Selznick, Philip. 1966. *TVA and the Grass Roots*. New York: Harper & Row.

Southern Development Bancorporation [Southern]. 1988. Planning document, April 18.

Styne, Jule, and Leo Robin. 1953. *Gentlemen Prefer Blondes*. Twentieth-Century Fox.

Taub, Richard. 1984. *Paths of Neighborhood Change: Race and Crime in Urban America*. Chicago: University of Chicago Press.

———. 1988. *Community Capitalism*. Boston: Harvard Business School Press.

———. 1989. *Entrepreneurship in India's Small-Scale Industries*. Riverdale, MD: Riverdale Company.

———. 1990. Nuance and Meaning in Community Development: Finding Community and Development. New York: Community Development Research Center, Graduate School of Management and Urban Policy, New School for Social Research.

————. 1994. The Southern Development Bancorporation: Lessons
    Learned: First Five Years. Paper presented at the American
    Agricultural Law Association Conference, Memphis, Tennessee.
Wright, Gavin. 1986. *Old South, New South: Revolutions in the Southern
    Economy since the Civil War.* New York: Basic Books.

Index

Note: A page number with a *t* refers to a table or chart and *m* refers to a map.

AEG. *See* Arkansas Enterprise Group (AEG)

AEG Manufacturing Services (AMS): advertising campaign, 51; functional organization of, 23*t*; funding for, 78; goals of, 118–19; investments in Helena, 60, 107; lender liability and, 70; lending and technical assistance from, 76–80, 127; mission of, 22–24; as part of Southern, 19; pressure to be self-sustaining, 79; staff of, 122; successes/failures, 79–80; use of leverage, 117, 118; working capital investments concept, 74–76

African Americans: of Arkadelphia, 15, 43, 56–57; banking practices concerning, 7, 70; generation of loans to, 33, 125–27; lack of access to credit, 6–7; of Pine Bluff, 26; as poster children for Southern, 53; problems with lending to/investing in, 72–73, 130–31; South Shore Bank program for, 8–9; as target population for Southern, 33; wariness of Southern, 86

AIDC. *See* Arkansas Industrial Development Commission (AIDC)

AMS. See AEG Manufacturing Services (AMS)

Arkadelphia, Arkansas: advantages/disadvantages of for Southern, 14–16, 25–26; attraction of industry, 62; county data, 59*t*; Elk

Horn Bank's impact on, 109–10; infrastructure development in, 63; knowledge of Southern in, 50*t*, 50–51; labor issues in, 64; leadership of, 124–25; local perception of community/leaders, 106*t*; perception of Southern, 41; pressure toward minority deals in, 122; renovation of downtown, 99–101; as target area, 56–57, 58*m*

Arkansas: diagnosis of problem in, 6–7, 30, 49–71, 54–70, 71; economic status, 2–3, 3*t*, 14, 56*t*; economic success stories in, 3–6; localism/outsider wariness in, 13, 28–31, 36, 40–41, 52, 116; median household income, 2; target areas, 57, 58*m*, 59–60

Arkansas Development Finance Authority, 82, 123

Arkansas Enterprise Group (AEG): approach of leadership, 37–38; catalyst activities, 129; functional organization of, 22, 23*t*; funding for, 24, 78, 79–80; legal issues, 19, 68–70, 112; loans from, 76–80; message to potential borrowers, 53; mission of, 22, 24, 65–66; as not-for-profit company, 17–19; pressure to be self-sustaining, 24; search for borrowers, 72, 129; staff of, 27; structure of, 18*t*, 65–67; technical assistance from, 19, 68–70, 76–80; as tenant of Enterprise Center, 100–101; working capital investments concept, 74–75. *See also* Arkansas Manufacturing Services (AMS); Good Faith Fund; Southern